JEREMY SAMS

Jeremy Sams' writing credits include *A Damsel in Distress* (Chichester Festival Theatre), *Chitty Chitty Bang Bang* (West End and Broadway), the musical *Amour* (Broadway), and Andrew Lloyd Webber's *The Wizard of Oz* (West End and Toronto). He has translated many works for the stage, and has worked widely as a musical director, and composer for stage and screen.

JOHN ESMONDE AND BOB LARBEY

John Esmonde and Bob Larbey together wrote some of the most successful British comedy series of the 1970s and 1980s. Together they wrote *Mulberry* (BBC, 1992–93), *Ever Decreasing Circles* (BBC, 1986–91), *Brush Strokes* (BBC, 1984–89), *Now and Then* (LWT, 1983–84), *The Good Life* (BBC, 1975–78) and *The Other One* (BBC, 1977–79).

T0346947

Jeremy Sams

THE GOOD LIFE

Based upon the TV series by
John Esmonde and Bob Larbey

NICK HERN BOOKS

London

www.nickhernbooks.co.uk

A Nick Hern Book

This stage adaptation of *The Good Life* first published in Great Britain in 2021 as a paperback original by Nick Hern Books Limited, The Glasshouse, 49a Goldhawk Road, London W12 8QP

The Good Life copyright © 2021 Jeremy Sams
The Good Life original TV scripts copyright © The Estates of John Esmonde and Bob Larbey

Jeremy Sams has asserted his moral right to be identified as the author of this stage adaptation

Cover photograph of Preeya Kalidas, Rufus Hound, Sally Tatum and Dominic Rowan by Michael Wharley; design by Shaun Webb Design

Designed and typeset by Nick Hern Books, London
Printed in the UK by Mimeo Ltd, Huntingdon, Cambridgeshire PE29 6XX

A CIP catalogue record for this book is available from the British Library

ISBN 978 1 83904 033 7

The Good Life was first produced by Fiery Angel and opened at Theatre Royal Bath on 7 October 2021, before touring the UK. The cast and creative team was as follows:

TOM GOOD	Rufus Hound
MARGO LEADBETTER	Preeya Kalidas
JERRY LEADBETTER	Dominic Rowan
BARBARA GOOD	Sally Tatum
SIR/HARRY THE PIGMAN/	
POLICEMAN/DR JOE	Nigel Betts
FELICITY/MILKWOMAN/	
MARY	Tessa Churchard

Understudies

MARGO/BARBARA/FELICITY/	
MILKWOMAN/MARY	Charlotte Bloomsbury
TOM/JERRY/SIR/HARRY/	
POLICEMAN/DR JOE	Oliver Hewett

Director and Adapter	Jeremy Sams
Set and Costume Designer	Michael Taylor
Lighting Designer	Mark Henderson
Sound Designer	Fergus O'Hare
Casting Director	Ginny Schiller CDG
Associate Director	Joanna Bowman
Composer	Tim Sutton
Movement Director	Jane McMurtrie
Geraldine Designed	
and Built by	Leigh Cranston
Puppet Consultant	Matthew Forbes

Production Manager	Sam Paterson
Costume Supervisor	Hilary Lewis
Props Supervisor	Lily Mollgaard
	Chris Lake
Company Stage Manager	Sarah Yelland
Deputy Stage Manager	Hazel McDougall
Assistant Stage Manager	Rosie Bannister
Tech Assistant Stage Manager	Cormac O'Brien
Head of Wardrobe	Natasha Hancock
General Manager	Fiery Angel

Characters

TOM GOOD
BARBARA GOOD
MARGO LEADBETTER
JERRY LEADBETTER
'SIR' aka ANDREW FERGUSON, *also plays* HARRY THE
    PIGMAN, POLICEMAN *and* DR JOE
FELICITY FERGUSON, *also plays* MARGARET THE
    SECRETARY, MILKWOMAN *and* MARY THE
    RECEPTIONIST

The play is in four acts.

ACT ONE
1976, Summer
Goods' House – later Leadbetters' House

ACT TWO
1976, Autumn
Scene One – Goods' house
Scene Two – Leadbetters' house

ACT THREE
1976, Christmas
Goods' house

ACT FOUR – Postlude
1977, Summer
Leadbetters' house

*This text went to press before the end of rehearsals and so may
differ slightly from the play as performed.*

ACT ONE

'Beginnings'

1976, Summer

We hear Lord Kitchener singing 'Life Begins at 40'.

Lights up on BARBARA *in pyjamas, joke wig (complete with tiara) and feather boa putting the finishing touches to a birthday breakfast. Enter* TOM *in his shirtsleeves. She can put a glittery conical hat on him and blow a serenade on a party horn, maybe a chorus of 'Happy Birthday' on a kazoo.*

BARBARA. HAPPY BIRTHDAY!

Champagne? Fresh from the vineyards of Asti Spumante! Via Peter Dominic.

TOM. The perfect breakfast wine.

BARBARA *opens and pours the wine.*

BARBARA. Open your card, ingrate. Shall I flambé the bacon?

TOM. Why change the habit of a lifetime?

BARBARA *busies herself with breakfast.*

(Reads the front of handmade card.) 'Roses are red, violets are blue. Mozart was dead by forty. *(Opens the card.)* Why aren't you?' Hag from hell.

BARBARA. You called, sir? There's more.

TOM. I was worried there might be. *(Reads.)* 'You had plenty at twenty. You were dirty at thirty. Will you be naughty at forty?' Very good, and, yes, play your cards right. Early night tonight?

BARBARA *(bringing food to the table)*. Your birthday treat. Never miss a year.

TOM. You're very kind to an old man.

BARBARA. Birthdays and Christmas, that's the rule.

TOM. And look on the bright side, I might still be nifty at fifty! I remember when I was at school we'd think how amazing it would be to be married. It meant you could have it off every night.

BARBARA. 'Have it off'? Charming.

TOM. That's what we used to say.

BARBARA. Well let's have this off... (*Removing a dish cover with a flourish.*) Da-da... Birthday cornflakes with added... (*Sprinkles from a teacup.*) hundreds and thousands.

TOM. Yay. Why are they called that though? I mean which is it, hundreds or thousands? Surely one includes the other.

BARBARA. Good point. If slightly dull. Okay. Birthday candles, now? Later?

TOM. Or perhaps it means there are literally hundreds and thousands. Does someone count?

BARBARA. Still quite dull. But if they do, they'd be right at home at...

TOM. At JJM, you're right. One of the bean-counting whippersnappers would be spot on for that job.

BARBARA. Now come on. It's not that bad.

TOM. No, you come on. And it is. Worse.

BARBARA. No, darling. Please not today.

TOM. And yes today of all days. I'm now officially past it. I used to be a promising artist, remember. Well, a promising art student.

BARBARA. And me. Promising piano student.

TOM. And now look at us.

BARBARA. Come on. Candles, Tom. Jerry will be tooting *tout de suite*. We have four candles. One for each decade.

TOM. How did we get stuck in this life? Me designing plastic toys to put in cereal packets. (*Panicked.*) My God, there's not one in here, is there?

BARBARA. I fished it out. Didn't want to traumatise you.

TOM. Baking Powder Submarine?

BARBARA. Brightly Coloured Dinosaur.

TOM. That's what I've come to. Scarlet Stegosauruses. That's me. And you, teaching madwomen the piano.

BARBARA. Mrs Smith is not mad.

TOM. Barbara. Did you know...

BARBARA. Bad, certainly... I've got her this afternoon.

TOM. Barbara, listen.

BARBARA. We've been on the same piece for seven months.

TOM (*insistent*). Did you know that after the age of forty the body starts running down?

BARBARA. Tom. Have you been at the *Reader's Digest* again?

TOM. It's a known fact. From now on, two million cells a day drop off like dandruff and they're not replaced, not ever. I'm over the hill, and rapidly careering down the other side. Life begins to *end* at forty! Lord Kitchener never sang that.

BARBARA. Is there any particular part of the body they disappear from first? Just asking.

TOM. It's not that I'm feeling old, I'm not. It's just that I'm now officially *old*. And what have I achieved? I mean really? After all these years, I'm still looking for 'it'.

BARBARA. I promised – later tonight.

TOM. No, not that 'it'. I mean 'it' as in 'IT'. The 'it' people mean when say 'I've got it' or when they say 'That's it.' That 'it'. IT.

BARBARA. I've no idea what you're talking about. Sounds like Morse code. (*A thought.*) My God, you're not getting broody are you?

TOM. I'm just taking stock.

We hear a rhythmical car horn outside.

(*Irritated.*) Oh, for God's sake. Why's bloody Jerry so bloody merry? Damn the man.

BARBARA. Okay, not broody, just moody. Eat up. It's drizzle cake.

TOM. Possibly the least appetising name for any cake, ever.

One more honk.

BARBARA. There you go. Ask not for whom the Volvo sounds…

TOM. How is it that only Jerry honks like that?

BARBARA. It sounds for thee, mate. Come on.

TOM. He'll be all huffed up. Big meeting today. Exciting new campaign. Sir's announcing some world-domination nonsense… the yes-man whippersnappers will be lapping it up. Olly from the Poly, and Smarmy Barney and Cuthbert Dibble and Grubb. It's a young man's game, advertising – how I am still in it?

BARBARA. Well Jerry likes it.

TOM. Jerry likes the dosh and the Volvo and bossing me about and taking all the credit. But what's his purpose, what's his *philosophy*?

BARBARA. I'll ask him. And I for one don't mind the dosh.

TOM (*drinking*). All hail the dosh!

BARBARA. How else can we pay for everything?

TOM. But what is it we pay for? There's not much mortgage, thanks to Great-Aunt Daisy.

BARBARA. I sometimes think she was the only reason you married me.

TOM. No, she was.

Car horn again, twice this time.

Come on, *what*? What do we have to pay for?

BARBARA. Well… there's heating, and food, and the rates, and the car…

TOM....which hasn't gone for months.

BARBARA....And the odd posh frock, the hols, the Asti.

TOM. Hang on, let me make a list. Can I use this? (*Takes the birthday card and a pen.*)

BARBARA. Don't make a list of our life, Tom. Get dressed.

JERRY *enters. Dressed for work. Impatiently jingling his car keys.*

TOM. Right. Here we go. Sainsbury's. Peter Dominic's. Macfisheries. British Gas. GPO. Millets. Hello, Jerry. Austin Reed. Dorothy Perkins. TV licence. Cornwall...

TOM *exits, still making his list.*

JERRY. What's wrong with him? We're late.

BARBARA. He's stock-taking.

JERRY. Well, I wish he'd hurry up, the engine's running. Oh. Do you want a shufti at the new Volvo 265? It's a beauty, leather seats, and a six-cylinder... (*Looking around at all the 'Happy Birthday' paraphernalia.*) Ah. Ah. Is it his birthday?

BARBARA. It's like a sixth sense with you, isn't it, Jerry?

JERRY. I'll get him a lager and lime at lunch.

BARBARA. You're all heart, Jerry. And do stop looking down my front.

JERRY. I wasn't. Was I?

BARBARA. A bit. Have some birthday cake. Tom's having a slight mid-life crisis, that's all.

BARBARA *begins to clear up.*

JERRY. What brought that on?

BARBARA. I don't know. Mid-life?

JERRY. Well his timing's terrible. I need him all chipper today. It's the Big Push!

BARBARA. Sounds like Passchendaele.

JERRY. That's exactly what it's like. Sir blows a whistle and we all scramble. Can I have a swig of this?

JERRY *drinks deep.*

BARBARA. So, what's your philosophy, Jerry?

JERRY. Of what?

BARBARA. Oh, you know, life, work, that kind of thing...

JERRY. Oh, I don't know. Never thought about it much.

BARBARA. Oh come on.

JERRY. Okay, then. Here's the Gospel according to Jerry. Suck it up, rake it in, and leave your work at the office. That's pretty much it. Oh and golf on Sundays. (*Thinks.*) Oh, and keeping Margo happy, of course. (*Thinks.*) Actually that's the main thing, come to think of it...

TOM *enters, now fully dressed for work, still writing, using his briefcase to support the card he is writing on.* JERRY *stares at him.*

TOM. Christmas presents for Margo and Jerry, birthday presents for Margo and Jerry, the Taj Mahal, the Star of Peking, the lions of Longleat, Freeman Hardy and Willis, WH Smith, Dewhurst's, Woolies, Odeons one, two and three, Allders and Timothy Whites, hello, Jerry, ready?

JERRY. Are you all right?

TOM. Me? Never better. Oh yes, and the Midland Bank. Bye, darling. See you later.

BARBARA. Yes, darling. And early night, remember?

TOM. How could I forget?

JERRY (*to* TOM, *raffishly*). Oh I see, it's *Sportsnight* with Coleman tonight, is it? Lucky you, Tom, I mean lucky both of you, I mean... anyway come on we're late. Moulded plastics wait for no man. Bye, Barbara...

TOM *and* JERRY *exit, leaving* BARBARA *slightly bewildered. She clears the rest of the table, switching on the radio as she passes. It's Andy Williams, singing 'What Are You*

Doing the Rest of Your Life?' She changes channel… Cilla Black singing 'What's It All About, Alfie?' Changes it one more time, this time it's Tony Bennett singing 'The Good Life'.

BARBARA *listens for a bit. Looks at her watch.*

BARBARA. Okay. Dressed. Dry-cleaners'. Library books. Undies for tonight…

She turns off the radio. Rushes out. We segue to 'sitcom' time-passing music.

Almost immediately BARBARA *(quick-changed) re-enters, fully dressed, coat, wearing glasses. She is totally engrossed in a book she has got from the library. Maybe some shopping. She slumps down in a chair – still reading. It's later.*

Right, cup of tea. And then… and then…

She turns on the radio again as she puts on the kettle to make a cup of tea, and some toast – all of this while still reading the book. On the radio is The Archers. *A storyline about animal husbandry…*

RADIO. It's lambing time and Phil Archer is rushed off his feet…

BARBARA *looks up, listens, and then turns back to her book (she's already halfway through it) as she waits for the kettle to boil.* The Archers *theme, and episode continues…*

BARBARA. And then…

MARGO *(off)*. Yoo-hoo.

BARBARA. And then… Margo!

Enter MARGO, *in full tennis gear. Completely made up and* soignée. *Alice band in her hair. A couple of rackets in a case.*

MARGO. Barbara, it's Margo.

BARBARA. I can see that.

MARGO. I can't stay.

BARBARA. That's a pity. Tea?

MARGO. Just a splash. Do you have Earl Grey?

BARBARA. Only builders' I'm afraid.

MARGO. Oh dear. Just give me a cup of boiling water then.

BARBARA *is making her own tea. Turns* The Archers *off, while she's there.*

With maybe a splash of milk in it.

BARBARA. Right-ho.

MARGO. Do you have low-fat?

BARBARA. Only gold-top.

MARGO. So be it, oh and can you just dip one of your teabags into it – just for a smidge. Perfect.

BARBARA (*offering McVitie's on a plate*). Choccy bicky?

MARGO. Absolutely not. (*Pats her tummy, as in 'watching my weight'.*) Barbara, Barbara – (*Takes a biscuit and eats it as she talks.*) you'll never *guess* where I'm going today!

BARBARA (*taking in her costume*). Erm… Deep-sea diving?

MARGO. Don't be silly, Barbara. I'm going to the tennis club.

BARBARA (*as if a great mystery has been revealed*). Ah…

MARGO. Well one has to be dressed right. Anyway, there's a new teacher at the club. A Spaniard. Pablo.

BARBARA. He's not actually called Pablo.

MARGO. He actually is. And frightfully good, they say.

BARBARA. At what?

MARGO. Barbara! Really!!

BARBARA. Sorry…

MARGO. But, all right, he is presentable. In his shorts.

BARBARA. Margo, you trollop!

MARGO (*on her high horse*). Excuse me, I put a lot of care into my appearance. And I expect some return on that investment.

No disrespect, Barbara, but when did you last get an admiring glance.

BARBARA. This morning actually.

MARGO (*as if this doesn't count*). From your husband I assume…

BARBARA. No, from y– yes.

MARGO. Well I wouldn't say no to a glance from Pablo. Particularly since June.

BARBARA. Why since June?

MARGO. Oh don't be dim, Barbara. June. You know, June! June from the office. In the typing pool. New girl. June. Jerry mentioned her. I felt duty-bound to pop in for a look last week.

BARBARA. Oh, what's she like?

MARGO. You know… Young. Obvious. Well she's moved here, to the other side of the main road, and she's just joined the tennis club.

BARBARA. Ah.

MARGO. Not sure *how*, but she has. Tom must have noticed her. All the men have.

BARBARA. Erm… not that he mentioned.

MARGO. How is the birthday boy?

BARBARA. Well. Reflective is the word I would use. Questioning. Making lists of what we pay for – and wondering why.

MARGO. Whatever for? Tom does fine. Okay, Jerry does better, but he did get Tom a pay rise.

BARBARA. Five years ago.

MARGO. *Exactly*. But you're right, living here has to be paid for somehow.

BARBARA. But *why*?

MARGO. Why?

BARBARA. Yes. Why?

MARGO (*patiently*). Barbara. You know full well that if you live here...

BARBARA. What? In England? In the world?

MARGO. No, here, in this street... you know full well that there are standards to be maintained. We're not any different, you and I. We may read different newspapers, or have different views, but the point is that we're *neighbours*. We both have front and back gardens, and to be honest, Barbara, your ornamental border could do with a bit of a trim.

BARBARA. Yes, sorry about that.

MARGO. We don't let the side down. We make an effort. What do you mean 'why'? What sort of question is that?

BARBARA. Well, we do live on a planet. A planet that we need to look after.

MARGO. Nonsense, we live in Surbiton. And we have the Royal Borough of Kingston-upon-Thames to look after it – that's why we pay our rates. Oh, talking of which, the Kingston Players have decided on their summer show. And it's, guess what? *The Sound of Music*! So I'll need your help working on that.

BARBARA. Really? I mean of course.

MARGO (*sings*). 'The hills are alive with the sound of – '

BARBARA. You're not playing Maria?

MARGO. Not yet. It's tricky when the director's Jerry's boss's sister-in-law.

BARBARA. What?

MARGO. Well, you know the theatre, it's all politics. You remember Felicity, Sir's wife? – well her sister Prudence is directing the show again next year. Though God knows why after last year's *West Side Story* debacle. Anyway, quite plainly I should play Maria particularly after my Anita – but dear Prudence may have other ideas. And I'm damned if I'm going to be sixth nun from the left – so she may need convincing. Oh, other news, we're having upstairs redecorated.

BARBARA. Really?

MARGO. Of course. I desperately need more wardrobe space, and two upstairs bathrooms.

BARBARA. Two upstairs bathrooms?

MARGO. Well I don't want Jerry to see me before I'm ready to be seen, do I?

BARBARA. No, I suppose not.

MARGO. It's all being rewired and plumbed up. And then of course we have to have downstairs done.

BARBARA. Downstairs too?

MARGO. Well we can hardly entertain in a pigsty, can we?

BARBARA. Well, put like that… But, Margo, don't you ever want more?

MARGO. Of course – that's what I'm talking about.

BARBARA. No I mean more to life.

MARGO. Barbara. What's got into you today? Are you talking about children?

BARBARA. Not necessarily.

MARGO. Well don't. It's bad manners.

BARBARA. Have you been thinking about that?

MARGO. Children? Barbara, we absolutely can't, and that's that. It's just not possible.

BARBARA (*reaching out a sympathetic hand*). Oh, Margo…

MARGO. Not if we're having the house redecorated.

BARBARA. No, fair enough. Interesting, though, isn't it – what we talk about and what we don't. (*Suddenly serious and thoughtful.*) Tom and I, to be honest, we've never, you know, really tried, I mean we've never not tried, or rather we've never tried *not* to. But since it's never happened it just didn't seem, I don't know, *meant*. And if something's not meant, then… I don't know…

MARGO (*who has not actually been paying attention at all*).
Sorry, Barbara, I was miles away. What were you saying?

BARBARA. It really doesn't matter.

MARGO (*briskly*). Oh good. Thanks for the tea. Got to work on
my backhand.

BARBARA. That's fine, Margo. Anyway I've got a book to
finish. An amazing book.

MARGO. A book, eh? Lucky you, having time for books. Well
don't let me stop you – must dash. Pablo awaits.

We hear a bell.

BARBARA. Oh sugar, Mad Mrs Smith. I'd forgotten.

MARGO *exits with* BARBARA. *We hear talk in the hall.
'Margo, have you met mad, I mean Mrs Smith?' 'Hello. Must
dash.', etc.*

Transition music. Time passes again.

Suddenly TOM *bursts in. Carrying his briefcase. Slumps at
the table. Wine is still there.*

Enter BARBARA, *not seeing him. She hovers by the door as
shouts off to Mad Mrs Smith as she leaves.*

Bye. Bye, Mrs Smith. Don't worry, we'll crack it next week.
Keep plugging away. That's the spirit...

BARBARA *enters fully.*

That woman is stark-staring – (*Seeing* TOM.) Jesus, Tom,
you'll give me a heart attack. What are you doing here?
What's going on? It's half-past three.

TOM. I've left.

BARBARA. I can see that.

TOM. I mean for good.

BARBARA. For good?

TOM. Yes. I've done it.

BARBARA. Done what?

TOM. It. I now no longer design plastic novelties for cereal packets.

BARBARA. What are you talking about? Are you mad?

TOM. On the contrary, I've never been so sane in my life.

BARBARA. Oh my God. What happened?

TOM. Do you want the headlines, or the whole kit and caboodle?

BARBARA. Just tell me what happened.

TOM. Well… It's been quite a day. It started with us talking, you and me…

BARBARA. I know that, I was here.

TOM. Then Jerry, and his new Volvo, and then the coffee break. And me, stuck by the kettle and the Rich Tea with the whippersnappers. Olly from the Poly, Smarmy Barney and Brian from Braintree. And Olly handing round Player's No. 6 and going on about how he'd asked June out. 'June from the typing pool with the enormous – whoo!…' – except they suddenly stopped all that cos they spotted me, the old bloke, and of course I wouldn't know what they were talking about because of course they invented sex, so I make some lame joke like, 'I hear her speeds are pretty good.' And they all went 'No!!!' and 'Boah!' (*Vomit noise.*) and 'Tom, you randy old goat' – I mean, 'goat', fine, but '*old*'! – and then they generously changed the subject to cricket which was actually worse because suddenly the penny dropped and I asked 'Hey. Which team are we talking about?' (*Barney voice.*) 'Well – our team. The JJM Eleven. We're playing Acme Plastics on Sunday.' 'What do you mean? *I'm* free on Sunday! Nobody asked me.' 'Oh, sorry, Tom, we're okay. We've got an umpire.' (*On his high horse now.*) 'I'm sorry. I'm not talking about umpiring – I would like to play.' 'Oh sorry – we didn't want to bother you, I mean not at your –' 'Age', that's what they were going to say, 'Age'. (*To* BARBARA.) No don't interrupt me, they were. Then Jerry came in –

JERRY *enters*.

I thought to back me up, but not a bit.

JERRY. Dial it down a bit, old chap.

TOM. 'How dare you? I'm an all-rounder. You've seen my googlies. And what about that time up at Marlow, I made a few that day.' He was right back at me...

JERRY. That was ten years ago. You made one run... and you didn't bowl because you strained your back getting your one run.

TOM (*as if* JERRY *is somehow missing the point*). I played though, didn't I?

JERRY. Yes. You played, all right? Now, can we talk about Sir's grand scheme?

TOM. Would you therefore mind explaining to these children that I still play cricket.

JERRY *moves* TOM *away... to a more 'private' part of the stage.*

JERRY. Still singing the middle-aged blues, are we? Barbara told me.

TOM. Why should I be running a *crèche*? At my age?

JERRY. D'you really want to know?

TOM. Yes.

JERRY. It might hurt.

TOM. I don't care.

JERRY. Okay. Open wide. We joined this company, what, eight years ago, wasn't it? And do you know something? I was frightened of you then. You were a better draughtsman and had better qualifications. I was going to have to rely on pure cunning just to keep up with you. Still, I needn't have bothered, cos look at us. I've got an office on the sixth floor, and you're throwing hissy fits about not getting picked for the cricket team.

TOM. What are you talking about? You're good at your job.

JERRY. No, *you're* good at my job. You use one-tenth of your ability. I have to use all mine and what I lack I make up for with sheer bloody crawling.

TOM. So I'm deploying one-tenth of my ability?

JERRY. If that.

TOM. Good. That's my point. I'm wasting my time deploying it here. Jerry, we design plastic toys – how can you seriously make that your life's work?

JERRY. It isn't – it just brings in the goodies.

TOM. The goodies?

JERRY. Exactly – the good life. The perks. We live it, the job pays for it.

TOM. So we do things we don't really like to pay for things we don't really need?

JERRY (*who wasn't really listening*). Absolutely. It's a very simple contract. Now because you are at work, I need you to be working. And to be on-message for the Big Push. Plus, let's be honest, you're not going to walk into another job at your age, are you?

TOM. Excuse me! Tompkins at Glovers' made me a very attractive offer only recently.

JERRY. Not that recently – he's been dead four years.

TOM. God, has he really?

JERRY. You see? Your business mind is just like the plastic before it goes into one of our moulds – formless.

TOM. And then, as if that wasn't enough, there was the last straw – the meeting about the Big Push. Which actually only served to push me over the edge. Sir called us to the conference room.

'SIR' *enters with* MARGARET, *his secretary. He is older. A fake bonhomie about him.*

SIR. So. Big day. Welcome, all. Jerry, and... er...

TOM. Tom.

SIR. Quite so. And his gallant boys. The amazing team led by...
er...

TOM. Tom.

SIR. Quite so.

TOM (*to* BARBARA). And the whippersnappers all had their
notebooks out – biros poised.

SIR. So. Gather ye round, gather ye round. And fear you not, no
heads will roll. But methinks today is a big day for JJM.
These are exciting times...

SIR *refers to his notes. And continues to 'talk' – the 'volume'
on his burble is, as it were, turned down.*

TOM (*to* BARBARA). There they were. Sir and the Yes-men.
Sounds like a pop band, doesn't it?

BARBARA (*ignoring this*). What happened?

TOM. He droned on and on, pointing to people the yes-men
yessed like little yes-machines programmed only to say
'yes'.

Volume up on SIR.

SIR. JJM are thriving, I'm not denying it. We're thriving on all
cylinders. Aren't we, Olly?

TOM (*as Olly*). Yes. We are.

SIR. But – actually, are we? Is thriving enough in a competitive
market, Brian?

TOM (*as Brian*). Yes. Is it?

SIR. It isn't. Only a cretin would think that. (*To Barney.*) You're
not a cretin, are you, Barney?

TOM (*as Barney*). Yes. No. I'm not. (*To* BARBARA.) Except
yes, he is. They all are.

BARBARA. Tom!

SIR. And I for one refuse to go back to the dark days in which there were no plastic gifts in cereal packets. No siree! Do you want to go back to that? Jerry?

JERRY. Er... yes, that would be a bad idea.

TOM. Et tu, Jerry?

A dirty look from JERRY.

SIR. No, what we need to do is to double down, to consolidate, to not just soak up our present market share, but to... (*Etc.*)

TOM *turns* SIR's *volume down.*

TOM (*to* BARBARA). Et cetera blah-blah et cetera. Expansion this, saturation that, Common Market this, mutual trade the other... Till the big reveal.

SIR. And so without any further ado... our *pièce de résistance.* Our bid for global expansion. Our gateway to Europe and beyond. Will you welcome please... Thank you, Margaret. The Marsupial Range! Thank you, Margaret.

MARGARET *produces, with a flourish, a large piece of card with drawings on it.*

The Wallaby! The Wombat! The cuddly Koala. The Opossum. The Kangaroo!

MARGARET. And Joey. The Baby Kangaroo!

SIR. Thank you, Margaret.

TOM. Dear God have mercy.

JERRY. Tom... (*To* SIR.) This is really exciting. Who doesn't love a koala?

TOM. Bollocks. They're vicious little buggers. Off their tits on eucalyptus. (*To* BARBARA.) But then it was all on me. 'Tom can make anything lovable. Can't you, Tom?' 'Tom can bring them to life. Can't you, Tom?'

SIR, MARGARET *and* JERRY *join in here.*

MARGARET *and* JERRY *and* SIR. Can't you, Tom? Can't you, Tom?… Can't you, erm…? So what are you going to do, Tom? What are you?

This becomes, as it were, TOM's *nightmare/breakdown…*

Pause.

TOM. I'll tell you what I'm going to do.

ALL. What are you going to do? What are you going to do? What are you going to do?

TOM. I'm going to go to the pub. And I think I'm going to stay there.

As TOM *moves away,* SIR *backs off and exits in shock.* TOM *slumps at the kitchen table. Pours himself a glass of Asti Spumante.* JERRY *hangs back.*

So I did. And I sat, and I drank – (*Drinks.*) and no one talked to me. Except Jerry who popped in briefly –

JERRY *comes over.*

– and helped himself to my drink – (*To* JERRY.) Sod off, Jerry.

JERRY. Don't worry, old chap. I can put this right. Eventually. Leave it to me. I've explained you're under pressure. That you might have picked up diphtheria. That you need some time off. I even talked about AA.

TOM. For me or you?

JERRY. Very funny. Go home. We'll talk later tonight.

He takes another swig of TOM's *drink. Exits.*

TOM. But I stayed there all through lunch, till they chucked me out. And thought. And thought. And wrote…

He produces some scrawled notes out of his briefcase, including the birthday card.

…and reread what I wrote. On your lovely card. I'm a designer, right? A good one, right?

BARBARA. The best.

TOM. Well I've been designing something.

BARBARA. What?

TOM. A life. A better life.

BARBARA. Tom, darling, Tom. I went to the library today.

TOM (*ignoring her, and warming to his theme*). Lovely. But, you know I think we can do this. I think we can live with no compromises, no rat race...

BARBARA. No money.

TOM. Exactly! We'll break the circle.

BARBARA. What circle?

TOM. The hamster wheel. Doing work we hate to pay for things we don't need. I know you're going to ask me how to translate this into practical terms, aren't you?

BARBARA. No I wasn't actually.

TOM. Right, here goes. We quit work. No more marsupials. No more Mad Mrs Smith, and we become as damn near independent, as free, as...

BARBARA. Self-sufficient.

TOM. ...as, what's the word – (*Looking for the word, finding it.*) 'self-sufficient', that's it, as self-sufficient as possible. We've got bags of garden front and back, so we plough it up and grow our own food. And what we don't eat we sell. We keep some animals – chickens, pigs, a goat. I like goats. We generate our own energy, we recycle our own rubbish. We mulch. We design the things we need – I'll show you what being a draughtsman is really all about. I know what you're going to say – some things we can't make – right?

BARBARA. Right, but...

TOM. Some things we can't grow – right?

BARBARA. Right, but...

TOM. So we flog our surplus and we buy stuff, or we do good old medieval barter, I don't know. It'll be bloody hard work. We won't have much in the way of mod-cons, but we might even enjoy discovering what it is we can do without. You know that list I made on your lovely card – did I tell you that I love you, by the way?

BARBARA. Not today. But...

TOM. Well I do. Every bit of you, even the bits you don't. Look, I crossed most of the stuff off the list. We don't need most of it. We may want it, but we don't *need* it. And the rest we can do ourselves. So it's goodbye Sainsbury's and Dewhurst's, adieu.

BARBARA. Tom.

TOM. Yes, you're right, of course, we'll want the occasional treat – the odd posh frock, Asti Spumante – but they'll only be occasional so they'll always be a treat. So it'll be...

BARBARA. Self-sufficiency in Surbiton.

TOM. Yes, I know, it sounds ludicrous, it sounds preposterous...

BARBARA. It sounds terrific.

TOM. Yes, I know, you're right, it's just a pipe dream. I've left my job and...

BARBARA. I mean, yes it sounds great. Let's do it.

TOM. What?

BARBARA (*taking his hand*). Tom. We'll do it.

TOM. Have you even thought about this?

BARBARA. It's not just you who thinks about things, and yes I have actually, a lot. All morning and most of the afternoon. There was a song on the radio. Look, I got this from the library – it's actually called 'The Good Life'. That's got to be a sign. Our name. But it's a thing. They're doing it in America, why not here? I've even been making notes.

TOM. So have I. You too?

BARBARA. And I tell you one thing, it'll change the look of the street.

TOM. And Margo and Jerry will go ballistic.

BARBARA. It'll be worth it just for that.

TOM. So... we'll sell the car.

BARBARA. And the piano. I'll teach on Margo's. We can have chickens in the greenhouse.

TOM. And eggs every morning. And I know where I can lay my hands on a rotary cultivator.

BARBARA (*moving closer to him*). A rotary cultivator. That sounds exciting.

TOM. For the spuds. We'll plough the garden and scatter the good seed on the land. And we'll flog our produce.

BARBARA. We'll flog our produce.

TOM. And we'll get a generator.

BARBARA. A generator!

TOM. You can run it on the manure from our livestock.

BARBARA. Livestock manure! And no more electric bills.

TOM. And a mulching machine, if there is such a thing.

BARBARA. There is something slightly sexy about the word 'mulch'.

TOM. Mulch.

BARBARA. Stop it.

TOM. Mulch!

Throughout the next sequence they should be getting closer to each other, kissing, maybe more...

BARBARA (*kissing him*). I could never kill a chicken.

TOM (*ditto*). It's okay, I've got my Black and Decker.

BARBARA. And I'll milk the goat. Geraldine – the goat.

TOM. And we'll get two pigs, Pinky and Perky.

BARBARA. Like me.

TOM. Yes, perky, like you.

BARBARA. And you'll be chopping wood?

TOM. All the time. Non-stop chopping. Like Mellors.

BARBARA. Sweaty work.

Music begins. Grows.

TOM. Oh yes. And we'll make our own clothes, we'll get a loom.

BARBARA. I do love a loom!

TOM. With the wool from the goat.

BARBARA. From Geraldine.

TOM. We'll be poor.

BARBARA. We'll be broke.

TOM. There'll be slugs.

BARBARA. There'll be fowl pest.

TOM. There'll be foxes.

BARBARA. And potato blight.

TOM. I love you, farm girl.

BARBARA. I love you, peasant boy.

By now they are almost on top of the kitchen table.

TOM. Be careful.

BARBARA. Why?

TOM. Mind the birthday cake.

BARBARA. Sod it. Let's mulch it.

Music crescendoes under this and by now the Goods' house should be revolving off.

*We revolve into the Leadbetters' front room. It is night-time
and* MARGO *and* JERRY *are in their pyjamas and dressing
gowns with mugs of cocoa or Horlicks. There is some cheesy
music playing on their radiogram, 'Love Is a Many-
Splendored Thing' – or similar.*

MARGO, *her ear glued to the wall, is listening to the sounds
from next door, with a disgusted look on her face.*

MARGO. Have they finished?

JERRY. I think so.

MARGO. It's absolutely disgusting. They've both gone
completely insane.

JERRY. It's only a blip. I'll get him back into the office. I need
him back.

MARGO. I don't mean that, I mean the sounds they're making.
It's like having farm animals next door.

JERRY. Well, it is his birthday.

MARGO. Jerry. Drink. We need to talk about Felicity's sister.

JERRY *gets* MARGO *a tiny whiskey – a big one for himself.*

Jerry. Ice.

JERRY. Coming up.

MARGO. We need to talk about Felicity's sister and *The Sound
of Music*.

MARGO *notices that* JERRY *is not wearing slippers.*

Jerry. Feet.

JERRY. What?

MARGO. Jerry. Slippers.

JERRY. Sorry.

MARGO. Plus. How are you going to get him back to work?

JERRY. Who? Tom?

MARGO. Yes.

JERRY. Might be tricky.

MARGO. We can't live next door to the unemployed. It'll affect the house prices.

JERRY. He'll find something. He's nothing if not imaginative.

MARGO. Yes, we can all hear that, quite clearly. Jerry. Refill.

JERRY gets up. We hear a distant yelp.

Not again!

JERRY (*going to the window*). No, look, it's outside... they're out in the garden. Come and look.

MARGO. In the garden! I certainly don't want to look at them doing... whatever they're doing...

JERRY. No, they're not. They've stopped.

MARGO. For now...

JERRY. No. Look, they're running around like little kids.

We hear whooping and giggling from the garden.

Margo, Margo, they're in the pond. They're splashing around the goldfish pond.

MARGO comes to the window and watches, incredulously.

MARGO. My God, so they are. What about the neighbours? And those poor fish. Stop them, Jerry. No! No!! Now they're trampling on their ornamental borders!

They both look. Enthralled and horrified.

JERRY. What's he doing now? He's just grabbed a handful of roses.

We hear a distant 'ow'.

Now he's down on one knee.

MARGO. I really don't want to look.

JERRY. No, it's a bouquet. It's romantic.

MARGO. It's repulsive. (*Shields her eyes, but doesn't turn away.*) What are they doing now?

JERRY. Look, Margo, look.

MARGO *looks, between her fingers, in spite of herself.*

Look. They're dancing.

A pause.

MARGO. They're what?

JERRY. They're actually dancing.

MARGO. Ridiculous.

JERRY. Absolutely. (*Pause.*) When did we last dance?

MARGO. The Amalgamated Plastics Ball. And you got para-bloody-lytic.

JERRY (*taking her arm*). Come on, old thing, let's give it a whirl.

MARGO (*not undelighted*). Stop it, Jerry. I said stop it.

The music swells (Matt Monro, 'Let there be Love') and they begin to dance, slightly formally. As the lights fade we see JERRY*'s hand snake towards her bottom.*

Jerry! What are you doing? Look where your hand is. Are you ill?

Lights fade. The music continues.

End of Act One.

ACT TWO

'The Goat'

Scene One

1976, Autumn

The Goods' house. A few months later. Saturday afternoon.

The Goods' is pretty much transformed. TOM *and* BARBARA *are coming along nicely in self-sufficiency. We see various expense-saving devices. A loom, etc. Washing everywhere. There is a generator upstage. They are wearing home-made clothes, very peasanty in look. Headscarf and dungarees, plus a holey cardigan, for* BARBARA. *Farm clothes (flat cap?) with scarf for* TOM. *There are trays and wooden boxes of sprouting plants and vegetables everywhere. A couple of dustbins, doubling as vats of liquid.*

BARBARA *has a milk pail and a stool. And is milking Geraldine (a goat) – maybe real, maybe just real-looking… maybe we see enough of her to deduce 'goat'. She is bleating loudly.*

BARBARA. Okay. Okay. Come on, Geraldine. Work with me here – we talked about this. That's it. Just a little bit more for Mummy's tea. You concentrate on that end and I'll concentrate on this end. Just a bit more. (*As if, or maybe in reality, the goat has pooed.*) Oh, Geraldine! Good God. That's disgusting. Call yourself a lady? Geraldine, that stinks. Got to get this cleaned up before Daddy comes in. God, the pong. Geraldine.

Enter TOM *from the garden, he is shooing birds away.*

TOM. Shoo, shoo, all of you – I've told you before – get out of my garden. And stay out.

BARBARA. What's the matter? Pan's People after you again?

TOM. No, the starlings are after our seedlings again. Every time I turn my back... And yes very funny – (*Sees the goat.*) What? What's Geraldine doing in here? Did she get loose again?

BARBARA (*referring to the poo*). Yes, she did a bit!

TOM (*transferring 'poo' with a trowel into a special plastic bucket*). No, I mean why's she in here? She's got *Chez Géraldine* in the garden. She's quite happy in there.

BARBARA (*helping with the poo*). She may be but I'm not. It's freezing out... She's got a fleece. I haven't.

TOM. Not for long, she hasn't. That lot's coming off. For the loom. And Geraldine is worth her weight in gold. Wool to weave. Milk to drink and poo for the generator.

BARBARA. She's a goat among goats.

TOM. She's a godsend. How was the yield?

They look at the milk. Sniff it.

BARBARA. It's a bit pongy.

TOM. That's maybe more her than the milk. Get her out, will you? And tether her properly, farm girl.

BARBARA. Yes, boss.

BARBARA exits (slightly gritted teeth) with Geraldine.

TOM (*sniffing the milk*). Yes. That is a bit rich. (*Shouting off.*) I've got a surprise. I said, I've got a surprise for you.

BARBARA (*re-entering*). What? At least we have more poo for the whatsit. What did you say?

TOM. Did you tether her properly?

BARBARA. Of course I did.

TOM. Well she got out last week.

BARBARA. Maybe because you didn't tie her up.

TOM (*'caringly'*). Darling. Is it the thirty-six-hour days?

BARBARA. No. It's you being a bit of a knob.

TOM. Sorry.

BARBARA. And, okay, the thirty-six-hour days.

TOM. It won't happen again. Promise. No more knobbage. (*Trying to leaven the atmosphere*.) I'm not sure if Margo will ever forgive us. She was actually eating the hydrangeas.

BARBARA. Who, Margo? I am sorry I missed that.

TOM. No, Geraldine. (*Sniffing.*)

BARBARA. I'm surprised her milk isn't a bit more fragrant.

TOM. Jerry was very sweet. Dragged her over here by the scruff.

BARBARA. Who, Margo?

TOM. Geraldine. She was captured, trying to escape.

BARBARA. Like Colditz.

TOM. Maybe she was hoping to meet up with other goats at Surbiton railway station.

BARBARA. 'For, you, Fraülein, ze war is over.'

TOM. Well it won't happen again. Plastic cable – she won't gnaw through that.

BARBARA (*pointedly*). Particularly if you tie it properly.

TOM. Are you alright? You seem, a bit… you know…

BARBARA. I'm fine.

TOM. Sure?

BARBARA. Yep.

TOM. Have you got your thingy?

BARBARA. No I haven't – and I can deal with my own thingy, thank you very much. And oh look, it just happened again.

TOM. What did?

BARBARA. You. Knobbage.

TOM. Oh yes. Sorry. Sorry. Long days. (*Pause*.)

BARBARA. And knobbage.

TOM. Kiss?

BARBARA. Too cold.

TOM. Okay. (*Pause*.) Rub noses? No? (*Cheerfully*.) I know – this'll cheer you up. (*Conspiratorially*.) Look what I've got.

It's a churn. Wrapped, but still very obviously a churn.

BARBARA. Really, Tom, you shouldn't have.

TOM. It's a churn. Da-da! Now we can have goat's butter.

BARBARA. Can you make goat's butter?

TOM. We'll find out in a minute.

BARBARA (*handing him a jar of goat's milk*). Here you go. One I prepared earlier.

TOM. Thank you, Fanny Craddock. Tell you what, you do the churning and I'll get the poppy-seed cake ready for the oven. Then tea.

BARBARA. Bossy boots.

TOM. Just maximising our time. And tea must be earned.

He deals with the cake mix. BARBARA *looks into the bowl.*

BARBARA. Still bossy. Are you sure about the poppy seeds?

TOM. Why not? It's European, isn't it. Poppy-seed cake? And we've got poppies. And we'll give it to Margo and Jerry, as a peace offering after the Great Escape. And keep some for us, obviously.

BARBARA. No, I mean, aren't they opium or something?

TOM. I jolly well hope so. We've got to find more stuff to sell. Why not drugs? Maybe we could grow pot – we've got a potting shed.

BARBARA. Shall we ask Harry?

TOM. That's today, isn't it! The Pigman cometh! Pinky and Perky back from their hols. All knocked up and good to go.

BARBARA. He'll know. Harry the Pigman. He looks stoned all the time.

TOM. Maybe we can grow our own, it's a cash crop, isn't it?

BARBARA. I think you need heat for that, don't you?

TOM. Ah, yes, heat. That old thing. Heat we don't really have, do we.

BARBARA. Not so much. It's all a bit 'pass the parcel' at night, isn't it? Take it all off, have a quick wash, then put most of it back on again.

TOM. Soap. There must be a way of making soap. What did people do before soap?

BARBARA. I think they stank. Do we?

She tries to sniff herself, while finishing the churning. This is a challenge – she decides to concentrate on finishing the churning.

Okedoke. Here we go. *Voilà.* Butter of goat.

They reveal the goat's butter. They look dubious.

TOM. Ah. Shall we try it?

BARBARA. Here goes? 'Scuse fingers...

They take a handful of sludge each. About to eat it.

BARBARA. Wait. Did we wash our hands? Goat poo.

TOM. Ah. We didn't. I forgot.

They put the goat's butter on to a plate.

BARBARA. We have been up since five.

JERRY pops his head round the door.

JERRY. Hello, peasants.

He enters. Full golf gear. Pringle sweater, tartan trews, glove in back pocket.

BOTH. Hello, Jerry.

JERRY. How's the Leninist workers' collective coming along?

TOM. Fine, Jerry.

JERRY. Are you rehearsing a dance drama about a combine harvester?

BARBARA. Very good, Jerry.

JERRY. There is a touch of Julie Christie to you, Barbara.

BARBARA (*giving a twirl*). Oh, do you like the look?

JERRY. Is Omar Sharif popping round later?

TOM. 'Fraid not. Just Harry the Pigman.

JERRY. Harry the Pigman? Oh for heaven's sake…

BARBARA. Yes, Pinky and Perky are coming back all primed and ready. Have you missed them?

JERRY. We thought you'd got rid of the pigs. Jesus, Margo's only just getting over the goat attack. She even talked to Mr Pearson about putting out barbed wire. I managed to dissuade her.

TOM. It won't happen again. We promise.

JERRY. The chickens in the greenhouse were one thing. Now the pigs. Margo draws the line at pigs.

TOM. You won't hear a squeal out of them.

JERRY. Actually, we've got guests this evening.

TOM. I promise I'll mute the pigs, Jerry. You've been very patient.

JERRY. No it's not that – we wondered if you'd join us. I'm doing golf with Sir, and then he and Felicity are coming round for supper – so we wondered if you'd, you know, like to…

BARBARA. We can't really. We wouldn't want to, you know…

JERRY. Margo's got one of her mysterious campaigns afoot. She says she needs your help. So she's planning a feast.

TOM (*politely*). Thanks but… it's just that… we don't really eat from tins.

JERRY. How dare you? It's not from tins, it's from the new freezer.

TOM. Well, we're more into eating our own produce. The bounty of the land and all that. Whatever the bloody starlings haven't snaffled.

JERRY. Look, Tom, Margo's machinations to one side. I've been working like billy-o to get Sir to come round to the idea of you getting back to JJM.

TOM. But, Jerry…

JERRY. Not, full time, just some freelancing. Just to help out. And it also would help me. We need you. The marsupials are an endangered species.

TOM (*in spite of himself*). Really? Well maybe if you tried…

BARBARA (*firmly*). Tom.

TOM. I mean there might be a way to…

BARBARA. Tom.

TOM. Of course. Tell you what, we'll pop round later. We've got some presents for you anyway. Some of our produce.

JERRY. Right-ho. Looking forward to sampling it. What's this? Looks good.

TOM. It's… it's…

Before anyone can stop him, he takes a spoonful of goat's butter.

JERRY. Ah…

JERRY's face is one of shock and puzzlement.

BARBARA. It's a work-in-progress.

JERRY (*after a moment*). Actually, it's not that bad. Butter, right.

BARBARA. Sort of.

JERRY. You can really taste the goat.

BARBARA. I bet.

TOM. And we'll bring some wine.

JERRY. It's okay, we've got wine.

BARBARA. Not ours you haven't.

She removes the lid from a dustbin.

Our very own Peapod Burgundy. We'll pop a couple of bottles round for later. Beware, it packs a punch!

JERRY. I like the sound of that. And, what, you both made all that – together?

TOM. Jerry, please, of course.

BARBARA. We do everything together.

JERRY (*impressed*). Like fifty-fifty?

TOM. Well the livestock lends a hoof, but yes, fifty-fifty.

JERRY. Well I think you're both insane.

BARBARA. Of course, but *equally* insane.

JERRY (*checking his watch*). Well, Surbiton Golf Club waits for no man. Tee-off at twelve. Got to make sure Sir beats me. It's a challenge, he's absolutely terrible. But got to soften him up, you know, for work, and for later.

TOM. Then shove off, Jerry. We're busy. We've got seeds to get in.

JERRY (*ribaldly*). I bet you have. So, you'll pop round after, then, I mean later?

TOM. Yes.

BARBARA. Probably.

JERRY. We all need a bit of time off, don't we? I know I do. *Adios*, peasants.

TOM *and* BARBARA *are left alone. Pause. They both slump.*

TOM. Is it?

BARBARA. Is it what?

TOM. Is it getting too much?

BARBARA (*rallying*). Too much? For me?

TOM. Is there anything you miss? Really?

BARBARA. No. Not really. You?

TOM. No. Well yes.

BARBARA. What?

TOM. Yes. Our 'Pagan Rites'.

Pause.

BARBARA. Yes there is that.

TOM. Our Saturday nights off.

BARBARA. Yes.

TOM. And our Sunday mornings in. The good old 'have-it-away day'. Driving up to a three-star hotel in Bucks or Beds or somewhere, sherry, cuddle, nap, three-course meal, drinks in the room, deep hot bath, telly till closedown, a bit of God-knows-whatting after, then deep deep sleep in a deep deep bed, all toasty and cuddly, then a long lie-in, then more cuddles, then... Barb?

BARBARA *has fallen asleep at the table.*

BARBARA. What?

TOM. What was I saying?

BARBARA. Something about beds. And deep. And I miss all that too. I can't lie.

TOM. Well, if I took on some extra work, we could still...

BARBARA (*suddenly alert*). But then I'd be doing more here, wouldn't I? And we have to be fifty-fifty, don't we? Like Jerry said.

TOM. Jerry, yes. Were you flirting with him?

BARBARA. Excuse me. I was more flirted against than flirting. It's what men do.

TOM. Well it's not what I do, and you were glowing.

BARBARA. I wasn't and what about you and Margo?

TOM. That's gallantry. Anyway, we need them. They need us. Who else are they going to patronise? Come on, let's just have five minutes to ourselves.

We hear MARGO's *voice.*

MARGO. Yoo-hoo.

TOM. Or maybe not.

MARGO *enters. Immaculately elegant. Carrying a posh-looking plastic bag, which, as we will see, contains a dress.*

MARGO. Barbara, Tom, it's Margo.

BARBARA. I can see that.

MARGO. I can't stay.

BARBARA. That's a pity.

TOM. Where are you off to, Margo. You look absolutely ravishing. A Bond Street gallery opening, surely?

BARBARA *raises an eyebrow.*

MARGO (*flattered*). Don't be dim, Tom. Just Waitrose. For tonight. We have guests. Jerry said you might pop round later?

BARBARA. Erm…

MARGO. Excellent. There's been a setback.

BARBARA. Oh?

MARGO. In my plans. I have spies at the Kingston Players. Valerie Pilkington is on the committee. And she's just called to say that they're about to announce the casting for *Sound of Music*. And it's wrong.

TOM. Wrong?

MARGO. Yes. The casting. It needs to be corrected. I seem to be down for Sister Sophia.

TOM. Who's she?

MARGO. Exactly. She doesn't even speak.

TOM. Perhaps she's from a silent order.

MARGO. Don't be facetious, Tom. This is important. They seem, for some reason, to be about to offer Maria to someone else. In fact, June, from Jerry's office.

TOM. Ah, June. She's on everybody's lips.

MARGO. I don't doubt it. Anyway, it turns out she's some sort of drama-school dropout and has just joined the Players. And this casting, obviously, cannot happen. So I'm going to insist on your help, Barbara.

BARBARA. Erm...

MARGO. Thank you, Barbara. Oh, and, Barbara, I almost forgot – I come bearing gifts. I have something for you.

BARBARA. Ooh.

MARGO *produces a brightly coloured dress from the bag.*

That's nice.

MARGO. Well, that's what I thought when I bought it. It was a mistake, however.

BARBARA (*looking at the label*). Pierre Legrand. Quite an expensive mistake.

MARGO. I'll tell you what happened. I got it home, I put it on, and I thought to myself, Margo, that simply looks cheap and nasty. So I wondered if you'd like it.

Pause.

BARBARA. Margo, you are the mistress of the unfortunate phrase.

MARGO. Oh don't be silly, I didn't mean that... I simply thought of you – and I know how difficult it is for you to look presentable with nothing to wear. And I saw the piano being taken away last week.

BARBARA. I haven't worn a piano in years...

MARGO. Barbara, you know very well what I mean. And did I tell you we've swapped ours, at Potters' Music for an electric organ?

BARBARA. Ah. Lovely.

MARGO. Which you'll be playing for us later? Yes? I have the music.

BARBARA. Well...

MARGO. That's settled then. And do take the dress. Surely *anything* is welcome.

BARBARA (*'Oliver' voice*). Please, miss, spare me a copper, miss...

MARGO. I was merely trying to be charitable.

BARBARA. Well when they have a flag day for me, put a penny in the tin, okay?

TOM (*saving the situation*). I think we should take it. It's a perfectly good dress.

BARBARA. We don't need people's hand-me-downs, thank you.

MARGO. Well, I feel totally humiliated. But I know my manners, and you are still invited to drop in later.

BARBARA. Thanks... but... (*She hears the doorbell.*) It's Harry, Harry the Pigman? (*Exits.*)

MARGO. It's who the what what?

TOM. Harry the Pigman. Quick. Margo, give me the dress.

MARGO. Tom, I knew you'd see reason. That's the best way to get it to her. Via you. And, Tom?

TOM. Yes.

MARGO. Have the bag as well...

TOM (*as sincerely as possible*). Golly thanks...

BARBARA. Come in, Harry.

TOM. Hi Harry!

> BARBARA *re-enters with* HARRY THE PIGMAN. *A large jolly chap. Red-faced. Stained apron. A cigarette behind his ear. He's affable and eager. As he enters the kitchen,* MARGO'*s disgust is palpable. She backs away from him as if he is contagious.*

HARRY. Hi, Tom, how goes it?

BARBARA. Margo, this is Harry. Harry, Margo.

HARRY (*wipes his hand on his dirty apron before offering it*). How do.

> MARGO *spurns his outstretched hand and pats her hair.*

BARBARA. The girls are in the van, Tom.

HARRY. All hale and hearty and shagged out, eh?

MARGO. Do you really have to adopt that tone?

HARRY. Excuse me. I'm just talking about the pigs.

BARBARA (*intervening*). Harry? Margo? Cup of tea? (*Gets some mugs, one for* HARRY.)

MARGO. Absolutely not.

> *She's trying to escape now, convinced she will pick up some terrible infection – but* HARRY, *a big man, still with an outstretched hand, always seems to get in her way.*

HARRY. You won't catch swine fever, don't worry.

MARGO. I've no idea what I'll catch. I'd really rather not find out. Bye, Barbara, bye, Tom, bye... erm... Mr Pig.

> MARGO *exits gingerly, giving* HARRY *a wide berth. He sits down with his tea.*

BARBARA. Tom? Tea?

TOM. In a sec, just got to put Margo's cake in the oven.

> *He pours the cake mix into a large baking tin.*

HARRY. You making a cake for her? That stuck-up madam? She don't deserve it.

TOM. Well, you know, neighbours, we all have to get along.

HARRY. Wouldn't even shake me hand.

BARBARA. We'll get the pigs. They're all caged up? You relax and have your tea.

HARRY (*producing a tobacco tin with several joints in it*). Thanks. You don't mind if I have one of these, do you?

TOM (*'hip'*). No! Cool, man! Go ahead!

HARRY *lights one up. A familiar smell fills the air.*

BARBARA (*to* TOM). You see. Told you.

HARRY. No, we all smoke these down at the piggery. Takes your mind off the pong. And pretty much everything else, actually.

TOM (*suddenly feeling 'square'*). I say. Harry. Here's an ignorant question. Do you grow that yourself? I mean, could *we*?

BARBARA. Tom!

TOM. Just exploring every avenue.

HARRY. No, and no.

TOM. Ah.

HARRY. But you know what, you can have one on me. I'll roll you a big one. A Surbiton Special.

TOM. I say, thanks.

HARRY (*tapping his nose*). And, listen, for the future, I do know a man who knows a man who knows another man, if you know what I mean.

TOM (*who hasn't a clue what he means*). Absolutely. And... thanks, old chap. For the, erm... You have your cup of tea, Harry. We'll get the pigs out the van.

HARRY. Right-ho!

As TOM *and* BARBARA *exit, she notices the bag with the dress in it by the door. She produces it.*

BARBARA. What? I told you I didn't want her cast-offs!

TOM (*grabbing it, and holding it next to himself*). Barbara. Give it here. It's not for you. It's for me. I want it.

BARBARA. Whatever for?

TOM. You wait and see.

BARBARA. I warn you. You'll look cheap and nasty in it!

They exit.

HARRY (*laughing to himself*). Ah well – each to his own!

HARRY *takes a large lump of hash, and is about to crumble it into a Rizla when he sees the cake mix.*

Stuck-up cow. This'll liven her up.

By now the stage is revolving away. Scene-change music. We see HARRY *crumbling a lump of hash into the baking tin. And stirring it in. And sampling a mouthful from the wooden spoon.*

Mmm, tasty.

Maybe we even catch a glimpse of the Goods entering with two pigs in cages, or wrapped in blankets.

Scene Two

Evening. The Leadbetters' house.

Which we now see in its full glory. There is a dining room, seventies art on the walls, chunky lamps, etc. Modern decor, for its day – although the furniture is resolutely chintzy. Big flowers in big vases. There is a hatch leading to the kitchen, as well as a kitchen door (these will be important). And a door to the hall. Occasional tables, a sofa and, in pride of place (not far from the hatch), a Hammond Organ.

MARGO (*quick-changed*) *is in hostess pyjamas. Her hair now completely done.* JERRY *in a sports jacket. They are getting ready for the arrival of their guests.* JERRY *is sticking skewers of cheese and cocktail onions into grapefruit.*

The scene-change music has now segued into evening cocktail music (George Shearing, or some such).

MARGO. Why can't they milk their pigs or whatever they're doing to them, after dark, so no one has to see?

JERRY. I don't know.

MARGO. Why can't they get a dog like everyone else?

JERRY. Dogs don't have udders.

MARGO. Twiglets, Jerry.

JERRY. Or Twiglets.

MARGO. In the bowls, Jerry. Thank you.

JERRY *continues to put out nibbles, napkins, etc.*

And really! It's like living next door to travelling folk. We'll be getting clothes pegs for Christmas next.

JERRY. Well... to be fair they've baked us a poppy-seed cake.

MARGO. Crisps, Jerry.

JERRY. Yes, darling.

MARGO. Vol-au-vents.

JERRY. Yes, darling. That seed cake's oddly delicious. Did you have some with your tea?

MARGO. Yes.

JERRY. Plus they've brought a couple of bottles of God-knows-what.

MARGO. And that ghastly rooster every morning. What's wrong with a teasmade?

JERRY. Well...

MARGO. Sherry, Jerry.

JERRY. Yes, darling.

MARGO. If Tom's decided to have a nervous breakdown, that's his business. But I don't see why he has to inflict it on poor Barbara.

JERRY. Absolutely.

MARGO. Not on the organ.

JERRY. Absolutely. They do seem quite happy though.

MARGO. Don't be absurd. They are heading for misery, degradation and squalor. And we'll have to live next door to it.

JERRY. Well, that's why I've asked Sir over. Maybe we can talk Sir into taking Tom back. If not full time, then part time. It would help me.

MARGO. But Tom is coming? And Barbara?

JERRY. Tom's mulling it over. I wonder if he thinks he has time…

MARGO. Of course he's got time. But what are they actually doing over there?

JERRY. They're working very hard, that's what they're doing.

MARGO. Well, so do you, so do I, so do we. I mean, really, they don't need to make a song and dance about it. It's just the same as us.

JERRY. Well. Not exactly.

MARGO. What are you trying to say, Jerry?

JERRY. Well. Their division of labour is more fifty-fifty.

MARGO. Yes. Just like ours. Cheeselets, Jerry.

JERRY. Margo. Let's be honest, ours is more like eighty-twenty. And let's face it, I'm the eighty.

MARGO. I have no idea what you're talking about, Jerry. I look after this house and everything in it.

JERRY. Mrs Pearson comes in five times a week.

MARGO. What about the garden?

JERRY. *Mr* Pearson comes in *three* times a week.

MARGO. Well I organise the flowers...

JERRY. Margo, if the Pearsons had a daughter who was a florist then you wouldn't be doing that either.

'*DING-DONG*'. *Their front door chimes melodiously.*

MARGO. That's them. We will discuss this later. Straighten up, Jerry.

She exits, with a dirty look. Left alone, JERRY *takes a huge swig from the sherry bottle.*

(*Re-enters.*) Here we go!

SIR, *formally dressed, enters with* MARGO *and* FELICITY *– the latter slightly ditzy and fey.*

SIR. There you are, Jerry. All spruced up, I see. Not like you were this morning, hacking away in the rough on the fifteenth!

JERRY. That was unfortunate, yes. Thought I was going to beat you after that putt on the par-five. Ah well. Felicity!

Hugs and kisses. During the following drinks and nibbles are offered and taken.

FELICITY. Jerry!

JERRY. Did you hear about our round of golf?

FELICITY. I've heard about little else!

SIR *wanders downstage and looks around.*

SIR. Well, this is all looking nice, I must say. (*Looks out of the window.*) Great Scott. What's thingummy done to his garden? Looks like the Somme out there.

JERRY. Yes indeed.

FELICITY (*joining him*). And he's painted the greenhouse pink.

JERRY. That was Barbara. She says the chickens like it.

SIR. The chickens?

JERRY. In the greenhouse.

FELICITY. It's sweet!

JERRY. He's done all that in a few weeks. He's even got pigs. And a goat.

MARGO. A dangerously feral goat.

FELICITY. I rather like goats.

Eyes turn to FELICITY, *briefly. She seems to be slightly in her own world.*

Can I help, Margo?

MARGO. Thank you, Felicity, that's very kind. I'd love to have a girly chat. Sherry, Jerry...

MARGO *and* FELICITY *repair to the kitchen, to produce food and bottles of wine, some of which come through the hatch.* JERRY *tops up drinks.*

SIR. Good heavens. I mean when he was with us he was always a bit...

JERRY. Eccentric?

SIR. Well more than that. And that day he left. Leaving the marsupials high and dry.

JERRY. Well, Tom's a *friend*. And I think what he needs now is care and *help*.

SIR. I'm running a business, Jerry, not a psychiatric ward.

JERRY. He's the best draughtsman we've ever had. And maybe even a minimal input from him would tip the balance on, say, the Webber campaign.

MARGO *and* FELICITY *have returned.*

MARGO (*to* FELICITY)....but there is something else I'd like to talk about... Now, your sister...

SIR (*this has its effect*). The Webber campaign eh?... Well, I've always been fond of... what's his name?

JERRY. Tom.

SIR. Quite so.

FELICITY. I've always liked him. He seems sane to me. And fun!

MARGO, *meanwhile, has also been looking out.*

MARGO (*horrified*). Jerry, look.

JERRY. What, darling?

MARGO. Look, they've made a scarecrow.

JERRY. Ah yes, Tom said they were having trouble with the starlings.

MARGO. No, Jerry, look what it's wearing. It's the dress I gave Barbara. How dare they?

FELICITY. Well, it seems to be working. I can't see any birds.

SIR *laughs, uproariously. So do the others.* MARGO *has no choice but to join in.*

JERRY (*still laughing*). That dress would scare anyone off! (*More laughter.*) So, food, Margo, shall we start. What's on the menu?

MARGO (*clenched teeth*). Coming right up.

JERRY. You do the nosh, I'll do the booze. I think you'll like this.

MARGO *goes bad-temperedly into the kitchen. Food and wine is produced from the hatch and passed to* FELICITY, *who ferries it to the table.*

FELICITY. Ooh, garlic. On the bread? How ingenious. And lemon wedges. Whatever next?

JERRY *is dealing with wine.*

SIR. I have to say, Jerry, your approach game is getting a trifle rusty.

JERRY. Rub of the green, Sir, rub of the green.

SIR. I didn't think I'd trounce you so thoroughly.

JERRY. Trust me, I was as surprised as you are. (*Uncorks and pours Mateus Rosé and Liebfraumilch.*)

I'll leave the wines to breathe.

Gives himself a huge glass first, which he empties, before serving others. SIR *picks up a bottle of Peapod Burgundy.*

JERRY. That odd-looking bottle is from Tom next door.

SIR (*reading*). 'Peapod Burgundy.' Sounds disgusting.

JERRY. You've no idea.

MARGO (*entering*). So here we are.

SIR. So, what's this? Looks marvellous, Margo.

MARGO. Just a little hors d'oeuvre. (*Very French.*) *Avocat aux crevettes, sauce Marie Rose.*

ALL. Mmm, sounds scrummy. (*Etc.*)

MARGO. And this is a rather jolly wine from Portugal. (*To* FELICITY.) Just, as one might say, a few of my favourite things...

FELICITY. What do you mean?

MARGO. Oh nothing. Squeeze of lemon, anyone?

They sit down to eat – avocado and prawns. Mateus Rosé is poured.

ALL. Mmm, lemon, lovely. (*Etc.*)

As they eat...

JERRY. Anyway, I'm sure Tom'll be giving up this nonsense soon. In fact he's popping over later – did we leave the back door open, Margo?

MARGO. Yes, Jerry.

JERRY. So they'll just wander through, and maybe we can talk to him, you know, about being part of JJM again.

SIR. Who are we talking about?

JERRY. Tom.

SIR. Who's Tom?

FELICITY. This is delicious. How did you do the sauce, what was it called again, Marie Celeste?

MARGO (*mysteriously*). Sauce Marie Rose? Well, it's a mixture of ingredients...

FELICITY. Well it's delicious.

MARGO. Garlic bread?

ALL. Oh yes please. Mmm. (*Etc.*)

JERRY. Anyway. I'm sure it won't be long before he tires of living off the land.

Music begins. The Leadbetters' house begins to revolve off.

In the next sequence, the set should not stop revolving as we see, alternately, glimpses of meals at the Leadbetters' and the Goods'.

Music underpins the entire sequence.

SIR (*mouth full*). Who are we talking about?

FELICITY. Sounds rather fun to me. Like Marie Antoinette at Versailles. Can I have some more wine?

MARGO. Jerry. Wine. Now, Felicity, about the summer show... *The Sound of Music*...

By now the Leadbetters' house has revolved off, and we see the Goods at a more frugal meal. Salad, their lettuce, and an omelette, their eggs. Their rather weedy home-made candles are lit. A bottle of 'Peapod' on the table.

TOM. Well this is nice, isn't it?

BARBARA. Yes.

TOM. More Peapod Burgundy?

BARBARA. Don't mind if I do.

Wine is poured and drunk. It is strong stuff.

TOM. Woo.

BARBARA. Woo, indeed. (*Shivering*.) Warms you up, eh.

TOM. A bit. Still cold. (*Pause*.) It's a nice omelette, isn't it?

BARBARA. Yep, the girls done good.

TOM. And the lettuce is nice.

BARBARA. Scrummy. And our very own.

They finish their food.

TOM. Was it better than yesterday's supper? I mean even better?

BARBARA. Pretty much the same. Maybe a bit more parsley. And a bit less cress. But yes, pretty much the same.

TOM. Are you hungry?

BARBARA. Desperately.

TOM. Me too. Wonder what they're having next door.

BARBARA. Something rich and strange, I'll be bound.

TOM. Well, soon we'll have Pinky or Perky to look forward to. And one of the chickens will be for the pot, in a bit, so...

BARBARA. Tom. Talking of pot. Dare we...?

They are referring to the reefer that HARRY *left.*

TOM. Well, it's organic, isn't it? I assume... So...

They light up. Much coughing.

BARBARA. I don't know if that's strong or not. Not done this since I was at school.

TOM. The Croydon High School drug cartel.

BARBARA. Happy days...!

They puff. The revolve starts to move faster.

TOM (*more serious*). I could, you know. Do some freelance stuff. Say a day or two a week. That would make the world of difference. That would give us some space. You can't teach piano on a Hammond Organ, can you? And the Pagan Rites...

We are now revolving back to the Leadbetters'. They have finished their main course. All pretty pissed.

FELICITY. That was delicious. How did you get the garlic into those chicken breasts?

MARGO. It's an old Ukrainian recipe.

SIR. Ukrainian?

MARGO. From Kiev I believe.

FELICITY. And the asparagus… and the ratta-thingy. How did you get that out of season?

MARGO. One has connections.

JERRY. And a freezer. More Liebfraumilch, anyone? Felicity? We need more wine. And pudding? We have puddings.

He exits to get some.

SIR. So, how are filling your time, Margo?

MARGO. There's not enough hours in the day! What with running this home and the garden and tennis and pottery and the Players. And Felicity, I'm sure your sister has been telling you about *The Sound of Music*?

FELICITY. Well no, not really. That's more Prudence's thing than mine.

MARGO. I was just wondering how casting was going?

FELICITY. Oh, you know, apparently they're just mixing and matching right now.

MARGO. Really? I was wondering about Maria.

FELICITY. Lovely part. 'High on the hill was a lonely goatherd'.

MARGO. Indeed… Well… You know June. From JJM?

FELICITY. Yes I know June.

SIR (*raffishly*). So do I.

JERRY (*from the hatch*). So do I.

MARGO. So does everyone, apparently. Well, I was thinking, none of my business obviously but wouldn't she be perfect for Liesl? The eldest daughter.

FELICITY. That part's been promised, I'm afraid. Valerie Pilkington's daughter Peggy.

MARGO. Peggy Pilkington? She's got acne and a squint.

FELICITY. That will have cleared up by the summer.

MARGO. What, the squint? I would doubt that.

FELICITY. Well...

MARGO. No, I do think Liesel's June's part. I mean she's hardly a Maria, is she?

FELICITY. Well I think that's more Prudence's choice really.

MARGO. Exactly. And it's a tricky one. Maria needs maturity, maybe. Plus June is busting– (*Can't quite say 'busting out all over'.*) Well not exactly a nun... I wonder, when you're next talking to Prudence...

JERRY (*re-entering, with more Peapod Burgundy*). This is more PPB from next door. It's rather good. What are we talking about now?

SIR. *The Sound of Music.*

JERRY (*who knows nothing about this; to* FELICITY). Oh really? Have they cast it yet?

MARGO. I'm hoping to convince Felicity's sister – Felicity's sister – why can't I say that? – of something...

JERRY. And we have cake for pudding. Don't we, darling?

MARGO. Yes, darling, this one is from an old German recipe.

SIR. German?

MARGO. Yes, from the Black Forest, I believe.

JERRY. And do try Tom's poppy-seed cake.

SIR. Who's Tom?

JERRY. You know. Tom, from next door. Brilliant draughtsman, He might even help with the Webber campaign. And, I now see, pastry chef. Their seed cake's quite something, isn't it, darling?

MARGO. Very moreish. I've had oodles. Cake, anyone?

JERRY (*aside to* MARGO). What are you up to?

MARGO (*aside to* JERRY). Nothing... just playing a long game. You'll see. (*Out loud.*) Cake, anyone?

Cakes are organised– as we revolve back to...

The Goods'. The air is thick with dope smoke. They are also eating poppy-seed cake, still drinking. And paralytic with laughter.

BARBARA. Well at least she's the best-dressed scarecrow in Surrey.

TOM. Best-dressed scarecrow in Surrey. 'I'd like to thank everyone who made this possible. Worzel Gummidge couldn't be here this evening.'

BARBARA. But, Tom, how could you?

TOM. Well, waste not want not, and I'm sure Margo will see the funny side.

BARBARA. Really? When did she ever see that? When did she ever see the funny side? So, come on, focus, are we going over or not?

TOM. I think I'm a bit, you know...

BARBARA. I think you are too. And I think I am as well. (*Giggles.*) We'd better have some more poppy cake, that'll act as a buffer. A big buffer. Is that a word? Buffer?

TOM. A buffer.

BARBARA. It's yummy, though.

TOM. They'd better like it. It's our olive branch. And I've got another present for Jerry.

BARBARA. What are you going to say to Sir?

TOM. I don't know. Will you love me, whatever I say?

BARBARA. I don't know. Depends on what you say...
(*Giggles again.*)

*By now we are back at the Leadbetters' – Black Forest
gateau, rum baba and Tia Maria/Baileys, and the poppy-seed
cake. A stainless-steel cafetière of coffee. They have been
drinking the Burgundy and the poppy-seed cake is almost
finished. They also drink some of the Peapod Burgundy.*

Everyone is squiffy and high.

The revolve sequence ends here.

MARGO (*a little unsteady on her feet – at the cafetière*). It's
called a French press. And we push this down...

JERRY. Stand back!

MARGO. Like this...!

SIR. It looks like a detonator. Look out, everyone!

FELICITY. Duck!

MARGO *succeeds in pressing down the plunger.* ALL *cheer.*

MARGO. There we go. Success with the press. So, with your
coffee, we've got more Black Forest gateau... no takers?

ALL *do 'I'm full' acting and noises.*

More rum baba?

Ditto.

No? Well, we've got a little more poppy-seed cake.

ALL *cheer. The seed cake is a definite hit.*

ALL. YAY!!!

JERRY. And some brandy, if anyone fancies it, and Mia Taria,
Tia Maria, coffee liqueur thingy for the little lay-deez. But
there's no more of the Goods' Peapod wine.

ALL. Boo!

TOM *and* BARBARA (*off*). Yoo-hoo!

The Goods stumble in. BARBARA *has wine.* TOM *a couple of golf clubs (a pitching wedge and putter).*

BARBARA. Fresh supplies!

ALL. Yay!

TOM. Hello, Margo, and Jerry, we've got a present for you. Golf clubs. I've given up.

SIR. Oh, let's have a look at them.

TOM. Hello, Andrew, here you go.

TOM *hands the clubs to* SIR. *Who instantly starts to practise golf shots with them.* JERRY *joins in.*

TOM *(pretending to notice* FELICITY *for the first time).* And, who is this? Dolores de Río!

FELICITY. He remembers! Ramon Novarro!

They execute a few Latin dance moves.

When was that dinner dance?

TOM *(really gallant and attentive, kissing her hands).* Two years ago, only seems like yesterday. And you look just as radiant.

FELICITY. Stop it.

BARBARA. Yes, Tom, stop it.

JERRY. It's the Russian peasants from next door.

BARBARA *and* TOM *(Russian accents).* Hello!

TOM *goes up to* SIR.

TOM. Sorry to snaffle your wife, Andy. But we were the toast of the Amalgamated Plastics Ball.

SIR. Yes, indeed. Er, nice to see you again, er…

TOM. Tom.

SIR. Quite so, quite so.

TOM. Anyway. How goes, the cut-throat world of cereal toys?

SIR. Well, pretty much as you left it. When you left it.

TOM. Yes, sorry about that. Maybe not my finest hour.

SIR. Listen, erm…

TOM. Tom.

SIR. Quite so. Listen. I can't pretend Jerry hasn't been talking to us about you, and your, erm…

BARBARA. Barbara.

SIR. Your Barbara, indeed. And I've also heard all about your problems and your circumstances, and the goat. And I'm not a hard-hearted man. So I won't mince about the bush. There's a desk waiting for you at JJM.

TOM. Really?

SIR. Yes.

TOM. Has it been asking for me by name?

SIR. Don't be silly. Come back and join us. Even a couple of days a week. Think about it.

All eyes on TOM.

JERRY (*pleading*). Tom…

MARGO (*astonished that he isn't saying 'yes' straight away*). Tom…!

BARBARA (*suspiciously*). Tom…

FELICITY. Tom?

SIR. So… erm…?

TOM. Tom. Okay. Andrew. I've thought about it, and… thank you, but not in a million years!

BARBARA (*lovingly*). Tom…

She kisses him, they embrace.

JERRY. Come on, Tom, put her down. Listen to sense. It'd be a darn sight less work in the office than the work you're doing next door. Sorry, Sir.

SIR. Not at all.

TOM. Work? What we do isn't work. I mean it is, and it's endless, but this – the goat and the chickens and the milking and the cress – this isn't just work. This is our way of life.

BARBARA. It's an adventure.

TOM. It's exhausting, okay, the two-hundred-hour weeks are a bit much sometimes.

BARBARA. And the occasional knobbage.

TOM *and* BARBARA. But it's *exciting*.

FELICITY. I wanted to do something exciting when I was younger, but then I married Andrew, and that was that.

SIR. A wise decision...

FELICITY. Was it?

TOM. Okay. Now that's cleared up, let's all have another drink. And a dance.

TOM goes to the radiogram. And picks out some Edmondo Ros.

TOM. Edmondo Ros. Hats off, a genius! What do you say, Dolores?

He puts on the record 'Cherry Pink and Apple Blossom White'. MARGO desperately tries to move furniture out of the way to make room for inevitable dancing. Several bottles of wine, the coffee and a large jug of water are put on the Hammond Organ.

MARGO. Jerry. Not on the organ. Can we stop this?

JERRY. No, Margo. Too late. That ship has sailed.

TOM (*dramatically, to* FELICITY). Come on, Dolores, you're on.

FELICITY (*continental accent*). Take me, Ramon...

TOM dances the cha-cha with FELICITY. Expertly.

JERRY (*to* MARGO). It's out of our control.

MARGO. Mind the house, everyone!

MARGO is desperately moving furniture as TOM *and* FELICITY *career across the room.*

JERRY. Well, if you can't beat them. Come on, babushka.

BARBARA looks at TOM *and* FELICITY *in full flow, and has no choice.*

BARBARA. All right, Jerry, just this once.

MARGO. Jerry!

JERRY dances with BARBARA. *Nice moves, but not really cha-cha steps.*

(*To* JERRY *as he passes.*) Jerry! Not so close.

JERRY. Oh stop it!

There is a moment when MARGO *and* SIR *might have danced too, but it passes, and they jiggle embarrassedly, watching their spouses like hawks.* SIR *consoles himself with the Peapod Burgundy, and plays with the golf clubs.*

The music ends. Everyone flops into chairs.

The next track is slightly more sedate.

FELICITY. Woo! That wine has gone right to my head.

MARGO. And Jerry's. And mine. I know, let's have some more poppy-seed cake, soak it up. I think there's more in the kitchen.

She opens the kitchen door, to reveal Geraldine, her tether trailing… who, worryingly, turns her head and looks at us. No one sees Geraldine except the entire audience.

BARBARA. There's one more slice on the table. I'm so glad you like it!

JERRY. No, it's all out here on the table.

BARBARA. Yes, you're right. I'm glad you all like it.

MARGO (*shutting the kitchen door, concealing Geraldine*). I love it!

FELICITY. So do I! We need more cake!

All make a beeline to the dining table for more cake.

JERRY (*intercepts* FELICITY *en route, offering his hand for another dance*). Felicity, shall we?

FELICITY. I couldn't.

MARGO. You won't! Jerry...!

  MARGO *takes* JERRY *to one side.*

FELICITY. Is there more in the kitchen?

  She goes upstage and opens the kitchen door, and is about to go in. SIR *stops her entering the kitchen and leads her back to the table. The kitchen door stays open, no Geraldine is to be seen.*

SIR. No, you silly fruit, it's over here on the organ!

MARGO. No drinks on the organ!

FELICITY. I must have that recipe.

MARGO. Jerry, you will not dance with that woman! You've made enough of an exhibition of yourself already.

JERRY. Oh come on, Margo, be fair. She's the boss's wife. I don't fancy her. It's not like Barbara...

MARGO. I beg your pardon!?

JERRY. No I mean it'd be a duty, not a pleasure, I mean...

BARBARA. I heard that, Jerry!

FELICITY (*who has staggered towards them*). It's all right, thank you, Jerry, but I couldn't dance another step.

MARGO. Good!

FELICITY. I want to sing.

MARGO. No I want to sing. I want to sing.

JERRY. Are you sure that's wise?

MARGO (*threateningly*). Don't anyone move.

BARBARA. I don't think anyone can.

MARGO (*exiting*). Jerry, we'll talk about this later.

JERRY. I don't doubt it.

BARBARA. Tom, I've got it – the seed cake!

TOM. What about it?

BARBARA. That's why everyone's so 'woo'! The Pigman must have nobbled the seed cake! (*To* SIR, *very careful not to slur her words*.) The Pigman's nobbled the seed cake.

SIR (*golf club in hand*). I have no idea what you're saying. Jerry, Jerry, come here.

JERRY. Yes, Sir.

SIR. Jerry, have you got any balls?

JERRY. I'm sorry?

SIR. I said, have you got any balls?

JERRY. Excuse me, I stand up to her all the time, there is no question who wears the trousers in this house…

SIR. No, you idiot, I mean golf balls. Have you got any?

JERRY. Ah right, yes, somewhere. In my bag in the hall, I'll just… (*Goes off upstage*.)

SIR (*to anyone who'll listen*). I demand another go.

TOM. Be our guest!

BARBARA. Help yourself!

SIR. I demand another go.

JERRY (*returning*). At what, Sir?

SIR. At that putt I missed.

JERRY. Which one?

SIR. On the par-three.

JERRY. Oh *that* one!

SIR. I need a hole! Somebody get me a hole. You!

TOM *obliges*.

(*To* JERRY.) It was about this far, wasn't it?

TOM. Will this do?

JERRY. Pretty much.

SIR. All right then. Clear the green!

Space is cleared for putting. BARBARA *and* TOM *are loving this! A glass is laid out, as a hole.*

Well then… This is what I should have done.

He putts the ball towards the cup.

(*If he is successful.*) You see!

(*Or, if he isn't.*) Well, obviously the conditions are quite different.

JERRY. Yes but what about my chip of the seventeenth!

SIR. What about it?

JERRY. I'll show you. Tom, open the hatch.

TOM *obliges*.

Barbara, get me a sand wedge.

BARBARA. One sand wedge coming up!

JERRY. Quick before Margo comes back! Shut the kitchen door.

TOM *obliges*.

– this is going down the hatch!

FELICITY (*drinking*). Down the hatch!

BARBARA. Jerry, you can't play golf indoors.

JERRY. It's my house! I can do what I like. I do eighty per cent of the work!

FELICITY. Bravo!

JERRY. It was on soft grass. I need a tee. Give me a tee.

ALL. Tee!

FELICITY. TEE! With the sandwich?

JERRY. Tom. A vol-au-vent.

TOM. A whatty-what?

JERRY. Get me a vol-au-vent.

FELICITY (*finding one on a plate and handing it to* JERRY).
I've got one.

BARBARA. This is fun!

JERRY. No, this is serious.

(*Placing the ball carefully.*) Stand back, everyone.

BARBARA *and* TOM *move downstage, others to the sides.*

Tom. Catch it if it bounces. Ready, everyone? So. This is
what I did.

*He expertly chips a ball into the open hatch. (This may take
a couple of goes!) We maybe hear distant crashing noises.*

ALL *cheer and applaud.* JERRY *salutes his audience, like
Tony Jacklin acknowledging an ovation on the eighteenth
green.*

Just to prove it wasn't a fluke. Again. Stand back…

JERRY *lines up another ball. He is poised on the up-swing
when* MARGO *re-enters in full dirndl as Maria in* The
Sound of Music.

MARGO. The hills are alive!

BARBARA. Good God!

MARGO. Jerry, what on earth is going on?

JERRY. I'm having another go! Get away from the hatch!

MARGO (*shutting the hatch, definitively*). I will not. That's
quite enough of that. I will show you all how this part should
go. I will sing. Barbara, I want you on my organ, now.

JERRY *guffaws.*

Jerry, don't be filthy!

MARGO *switches on the organ and sets the music out, ready
for* BARBARA.

MARGO. Barbara, get over here…!

BARBARA (*looking out into the garden*). Tom!

TOM. What?

BARBARA. Look in the garden. Our garden.

TOM. What about it?

MARGO. Barbara. Now.

BARBARA. Look at Chez Géraldine. The goathouse. It's
empty. She's got loose again!

JERRY (*poised, to* SIR). Open that hatch!

TOM. Oh Jesus, Margo's hy-danger's in drangea… I mean…

MARGO. Barbara. Play. Now.

BARBARA. I can't, Margo, there's a domestic emergency.

JERRY. Hatch!

MARGO. Nonsense. I need to bring music back to this house.

TOM. Margo.

JERRY. Andrew, open the hatch!

SIR (*going to the hatch*). Righty-ho!

MARGO. I forbid you! Barbara!

JERRY. Do it!

TOM. Barbara. Margo! We have to go.

MARGO. What's that noise? In the kitchen?

Indeed, there has been the sound of crashing and bleating.

JERRY. Here goes! Open the hatch!!

SIR *opens the hatch. And Geraldine's head springs through
(and bleats, terrifyingly!).*

A lot of things now happen at once.

SIR *backs away in shock, clutching his heart.*

SIR. Aargh!

MARGO. Aargh!

FELICITY. Andrew!

TOM. Geraldine!

TOM rushes to the hatch and pushes Geraldine back in and closes it.

MARGO screams, and backs into the organ, colliding with it. The jugs of water and bottles of wine spill into the organ, it makes the scary sound of fusing. Lights flicker.

JERRY. Margo!

The organ starts to short-circuit. Sparks fly from it.

MARGO. My organ!

MARGO backs away from the organ as its noises get louder and more worrying. More lights flicker.

BARBARA. Oh my God!

JERRY. Look out, it's going to blow.

The organ suddenly EXPLODES, causing other lamps on stage to fuse… Maybe one catches fire. Screams all round. People fall onto occasional tables, smashing them.

BARBARA. You said you'd tied her up!

FELICITY. She's lovely!

BARBARA. You knob!

A lamp blows loudly. JERRY puts out the fire with a soda siphon. There is an obvious explosion in the kitchen, the hatch blows open and smoke billows from it. Screams, chaos, people falling over, etc. Music, meanwhile, builds. Edmondo Ros. Absurdly jolly. FELICITY stands, centre-stage, impervious, in the middle of this chaos and flashing lights, dancing the cha-cha-cha.

FELICITY. Andrew. I haven't had this much fun in years!

Another noise of catastrophic short-circuiting. And blackout.

Interval (and clean-up!).

ACT THREE

'Pig Nativity'

1976, Christmas time

We hear Christmassy music. Two months later. A Saturday morning shortly before Christmas. It's cold. It's still dark.

We are in the Goods' house, which is further transformed. A very basic Christmas tree (more a Christmas shrub), home-made paper chains, sprigs of mistletoe. The loom has gone, in its place there is an Aga.

There is a corner in the kitchen for MARGO*'s things. A little middle-class shrine.*

Dawn. A cock crows. Enter JERRY *in a dressing gown.*

JERRY. Jesus.

He turns the light on but nothing happens.

Jesus.

He lights a couple of the Goods' home-made candles and shivers. He warms his hands at the Aga, fills a kettle and puts it on the range. The rooster crows again. He opens the door to the garden and shouts:

Shut up! It's seven o'clock in the morning.

TOM *and* BARBARA *appear fully dressed, very chipper and bouncy.* BARBARA *starts dealing with the Aga and the generator and tea,* TOM *with breakfast-related things. They are immediately whipping into action.* JERRY *is bleary and soon slumped at the table.*

TOM. Morning, Jerry.

BARBARA. Morning, Jerry, how did you sleep?

JERRY. Terribly. Pigs squealing, goats bleating and it sounds like that rooster was at it all night. It's like *Animal Magic* out there.

BARBARA. We don't really hear any of that any more.

TOM. But we did hear the vans arriving and leaving through the night.

JERRY. Yes, sorry about that. But that's the price you pay for overnight decorating work. An idea that Margo possibly invented.

TOM. Only a couple more days, old chap. It'll be done by Sunday night – ready for Christmas. Then we'll all be happy.

JERRY. It was supposed to be done by Thursday morning. It's a bit much to come back to find your redecorated home a building site.

BARBARA. Will Margo be joining us for breakfast?

JERRY. Should be. I'm just making her a cuppa. She's been up for half an hour already. Not yet in the best mood. Do you have any Earl Grey?

BARBARA. She's got her own stash. It's in Margo corner. In the blue Tupperware.

TOM. It's a bit of a change for you, isn't it? After a fortnight away… where was it again?

JERRY. The Algarve. Wonderful. Golf.

TOM. And then a month in… where was it again?

JERRY. The Selsdon Park Hotel. Gone right downhill. But the commute wasn't too bad. And good golf.

TOM. Well we can't compete with that but we can rustle up a good breakfast.

BARBARA. Generator's going!

And indeed there is a hum, and a patchy light on the stage.

JERRY. Ah, a simulated dawn! Actually, the insurance people have been surprisingly understanding.

TOM. We meant to ask you, did you mention the goat, in the claim?

JERRY. Well once we'd told them about downstairs fusing upstairs and blowing up the new boiler in the second bathroom and flooding the whole house, we thought maybe adding a goat to the mix might have been pushing it a bit. Any milk, for the tea?

BARBARA. Not the sort Margo takes.

TOM. And about Geraldine. Again, we really can't apologise enough.

JERRY. Let me be the judge of that. I'm joking. All's well, and so on, but when nothing was finished on the finishing date, Margo made a choice. And when Margo makes a choice…

TOM. I know. Sorry to have missed that moment!

BARBARA. How did she put it exactly?

JERRY. Well, she was firm but charming. Like an Easter Island statue with a smile. The gist was that the insurance people should stuff the Selsdon Park Hotel and recycle that dosh into overtime and now three teams of interior decorators are working round the clock.

TOM. When's the due date?

JERRY. The deal is that it should all be spick and span and shipshape by tomorrow evening. And ready for Christmas. I hope so, for all their sakes.

BARBARA. Well meanwhile, we're happy to have you.

TOM. See how the other half lives.

JERRY. And Margo can keep an eye on the house. They're terrified of her over there. Plus there's a letter due that she's obsessed about.

BARBARA. Hope you don't mind sharing a room with a loom.

The rooster crows again.

JERRY. It could have been worse. Margo!

MARGO enters, dressing gown, face pack, hair in a towel. Not a word.

TOM. Margo!

BARBARA. Morning!

JERRY. Tea?

BARBARA. Breakfast?

> MARGO *takes her Earl Grey tea from* JERRY*'s hand, takes a handful of dry-cleaned clothes from Margo Corner, then turns and exits as silently as she entered.*

JERRY. She'll be down when she's done her face and everything else. It's like Captain Oates. She may be some time.

TOM. Splendid, let's crack on with breakfast. Supplies, supplies!

BARBARA (*exiting towards the garden*). Righty-ho!

TOM (*cracking on with breakfast*). This'll give the Selsdon Park Hotel a run for their money. We have our own toast from our own bread. Fresh churned butter, courtesy of Geraldine. (Sorry again about Geraldine.) But we have her to thank for fertilising the mushrooms – and the tomatoes, and here they are. And we have our very own bacon.

> *The bacon should by now be sizzling away. Nice smells in the theatre.*

BARBARA (*re-entering, with a basket of eggs*). And six eggs. Well done, girls.

JERRY. I think I heard them being propagated last night. That rooster really puts his back into it.

TOM. How's Pinky looking?

BARBARA. Busting out all over.

JERRY. Like June.

BARBARA. Exactly.

TOM. Wonderful. I'll check on her later.

JERRY. Pinky? What about Perky?

TOM *and* BARBARA. Ah. Perky.

TOM. That's Perky sizzling on the Aga.

JERRY. Gosh, it's all a bit 'red in tooth and claw' here, isn't it?

BARBARA. Tom isn't sentimental. Are you, darling?

TOM. Only about you. Right, we have eggs, which my glamorous *sous-chef* is even now breaking into a bowl.

BARBARA does so with a flourish.

BARBARA. Ta-da!

TOM. Thank you, Johnny.

BARBARA. Thank you, Fanny.

Breakfast is being prepared and eaten through the following dialogue.

TOM. Move that book, will you, Jerry. Make some room, there's a chap.

JERRY (*looking at a book he's moved from the table*). *The Morphology, Pathology and Gynaecology of the Domesticated Pig*. Sounds like a gripping read.

TOM. Look, mate, I've got a very pregnant pig out in the garden and when she starts popping I want to know what to do.

JERRY. I thought there were people called vets?

TOM. There are, but they present things called bills.

JERRY. Barbara, I suppose you'll be knitting little booties for the piglets?

BARBARA (*amazed*). Jerry! How did you know? How did you know that pigs had to have their feet kept warm in the first few days?

JERRY. What?

BARBARA. Yes. Many a true word spoken in jest – it is a fact, actually.

JERRY. You're kidding?

BARBARA. No, no. Of course, it doesn't always have to be wool – in the olden days they used to wrap the piglets' trotters in rabbit skins.

JERRY. Did they? Really? I'm astonished.

BARBARA. You're gullible as well.

Gotcha.

JERRY. That's a cheap victory. Anything's a cheap victory before nine o'clock in my book.

TOM. Mushrooms okay, Jerry?

JERRY. Delicious. As long as I don't think too hard about what they were grown in. Don't tell Margo. As far as she's concerned mushrooms come from Waitrose and that's that. And these eggs are superb.

BARBARA. Aren't they just?

TOM. We'll convert you yet.

JERRY. I slightly doubt that.

TOM. Anyway, while you enjoy Perky I'm just going to nip out and check on Pinky. Where's the book? And the gyney-kit? And I need the thermometer. (*Finds them.*) We reckon it's some time tomorrow evening.

JERRY. Same time as our house.

TOM. Yes! Double due dates! Exciting!

He exits, with the gear and the book into the garden. BARBARA is left alone with JERRY. Breakfast is pretty much finished.

JERRY. Barbara. I need to clear something up.

BARBARA. Thanks, plates, would be nice.

JERRY. No, I mean something else.

BARBARA. Okay.

JERRY. You know when I said I…

BARBARA. What, Jerry?

JERRY. You know when I said at that party…

BARBARA. That was two months ago… history.

JERRY. Yes, you know when I said I fancied you...

BARBARA. Yes?

JERRY. Well I don't.

BARBARA. Oh. Okay.

JERRY. Not at all. Not even slightly.

BARBARA. And isn't that what every girl longs to hear? But thanks for clearing that up. Oh, let's leave a plate for Margo, shall we?

JERRY. Not that you're not lovely, of course.

BARBARA. Aha?

JERRY. And fun and funny, and feisty.

BARBARA (*playing with him now*). All the Fs. Just not fanciable.

JERRY (*flustered now*). No, I mean yes, I mean no, I mean yes, I mean...

BARBARA. Jerry. Shut up. And come here.

A big hug. Enter MARGO. *Immaculate* (*slacks and blazer*). *She notices the hug.* JERRY *springs away...*

JERRY. Morning, darling. You look nice.

MARGO (*frostily*). Morning, Jerry. Barbara.

JERRY kisses her chastely and indicates that he is going to pop upstairs to get changed.

JERRY. I think I need to get, erm... Can I use the bedroom?

Silence.

I mean, can I change?

MARGO (*more in sorrow than in anger*). I don't know, Jerry. Can you?

JERRY exits to get changed.

BARBARA. Don't be silly. That was just a hug.

MARGO. I know. But there is definitely something going on. Not you, but someone. He's always interested elsewhere. I notice. And he's always off in the shed.

BARBARA. Well every man has a shed. Actually our whole house seems to be a shed. Bit of breakfast?

MARGO. No thank you. (*Starts eating breakfast, though, during the following.*) I found his 'male interest' magazines there – he said it was for the articles on vintage cars, but I'm not convinced.

BARBARA. Well, boys will be boys. How are the mushrooms?

MARGO. Surprisingly yummy. And the other day we were at a Christmas party. And someone suggested we all put our car keys in a fruit bowl. I thought that's not very hygienic, but then Jerry explained. (*Pause.*) Mind you, it was Epsom.

BARBARA. Look, nothing's happened. And nothing will. But maybe when you have a home you should be more attentive. Take a leaf out of our rooster's book…

MARGO. Don't be disgusting, Barbara. These eggs are yummy, by the way.

BARBARA. And anyway that's the way men are. Tom was saying only the other day how lovely you looked.

MARGO (*shocked*). Really?

BARBARA. Yes, absolutely.

MARGO. Ah!

BARBARA. But that's men, they'll fancy anything in slacks. (*Notices* MARGO *is wearing slacks.*) Sorry, Margo.

MARGO. That's alright. Is that what he said, really? (*This time flattered and delighted.*)

TOM *pops in.*

TOM. Tea towels.

MARGO (*purring slightly, patting her hair*). Oh, hello, Tom.

TOM. Margo. You're looking lovely.

MARGO. Really?

TOM. So, I think we're on. I think it's going to happen.

MARGO. What is?

BARBARA. What? Today?

TOM. Not just today. Now. Pinky. I think she's going into labour.

MARGO. Really? Are you sure?

TOM. Look at this, Margo. (*Handing* MARGO *the thermometer.*)

MARGO (*can't bring herself to touch it*). Tom! Where's that been?

TOM. Erm…

MARGO. Don't tell me!

TOM. And all the signs are right, according to the big bible. The temperature. And the fact that she keeps rolling her eyes and going 'oh blimey'.

BARBARA. Well I'd roll my eyes and go 'oh blimey' if I was going to have seven or eight kids.

TOM. Well, I think she might be cooked. I think it might be right now.

BARBARA. What? Right now? No! What are we going to do if there are complications? Pinky!

TOM. No idea – I've never been a midwife before. Look in the book.

BARBARA *exits.*

Margo, can you hold the fort, and get some water boiled, will you?

MARGO. I'm not sure I want to be any part of this. And I really need to see how the decorators are getting on, and the post will have come.

TOM. Nonsense. Come on. You know you like pigs.

MARGO. Well I like pork.

TOM. In that case think ahead. Come on, chop, chop. Water. (*To* MARGO.) Hurry up, woman, Pinky awaits.

They exit.

Pig noises, off. MARGO, *with mixed feelings about being ordered about, fills and boils a kettle on the Aga.* JERRY *comes back down. Weekend clothes. Slippers.*

JERRY. I just popped next door. All go in there. It won't be long now.

MARGO. Good. Now I have to boil some water, for some reason.

JERRY. What are you talking about?

MARGO. The pig.

JERRY. The pig?

MARGO. Yes, Pinky. She's about to 'pop', apparently. And I really don't want to be any part of it. Being here's bad enough, but that doesn't mean we have to join in. And Tom's a bossy boots. I feel for Barbara.

JERRY. No I mean it's not long now. For us, is it? The house. Soon. Christmas. Hug?

MARGO. I've seen you and your hugs, Jerry, and I have to say…

JERRY. What do you mean?

MARGO. I saw what I saw.

JERRY. Oh, come off it. That was just affection.

MARGO. Really? Well maybe I could do with some affection from time to time.

JERRY. Well we have our moments.

MARGO. You have your moments, Jerry – and sometimes they're not much more than that.

JERRY. Well, it's all been a bit up and down lately, hasn't it?

MARGO. That's more or less what I'm trying to say.

JERRY. We'll get back to normal. Being here with them, not next door, not in Selsdon, okay it's a sacrifice. But the whole house, top and bottom, will be finished and cleaned up and gorgeous by tomorrow night. They know the deadline. God knows, you've reminded them often enough. And then it's Christmas, and then we're safe. You love an old-fashioned British Christmas. Turkey. Queen's Speech. We've timed it perfectly.

MARGO. Maybe you're right.

JERRY. That's the spirit. All's well that ends well and all that.

MARGO. Then I think I might just pop back to the house to make sure the workforce isn't slacking.

JERRY. Margo, they're the best that money can buy.

MARGO. I should think so too.

JERRY. So be gentle with them.

MARGO. I have no idea what you mean.

JERRY. Sometimes people do even better without you chivvying.

MARGO. I don't chivvy, Jerry, I encourage.

JERRY. Very well. You can pop over, and encourage, if you must. But they're on a deadline, so please don't put your oar in.

MARGO. You coming too?

JERRY. Later, of course. There's one or two things I need to look at in the shed.

MARGO. Jerry!

JERRY. What?

TOM *rushes in, elated.*

TOM. Three! She's had three!

JERRY. God that was quick.

TOM. Triplets! Margo, is the kettle boiled? We need to sterilise things.

MARGO. It's on the Aga.

TOM. Quick. Quick. Come on!

MARGO. Is there anything else you might need us to do?

TOM. I don't know, Margo. It's all happening so fast. Just be here?

MARGO. I have difficult workmen next door, Tom. Frankly I'm torn. And Jerry plainly has matters to attend to as well.

JERRY. I don't!

BARBARA (*rushing on, super-excited*). Five! There are five... Two more. All on her own! Come on, Tom.

MARGO. Five? Isn't that enough?

BARBARA. I'll pass that on. Come on, Tom. She's not done yet. There's another one on the way. Oh come and look, Margo, quick, it's beautiful!

MARGO. Certainly not. That sort of thing makes me faint.

TOM (*calling off*). Keep going, Pinky. (*To* MARGO *and* JERRY.) *Marvellous*, isn't it, nature? I read two hundred and fifty pages on piggery midwifery. Old Pinky can't read a word so she just gets on with it. Margo, do you have any Champagne at yours?

MARGO. Not chilled, we don't. No fridge.

TOM. Even so. (*Calling off.*) Hold steady, Pinky. (*To* BARBARA.) Come on, Mum, we're on!

  TOM *and* BARBARA *exit, with the kettle. Pig noises off.*

JERRY. It's cold enough in there to chill anything. Mind you it's cold enough in here. It might even snow.

MARGO. How can they actually live like this?

  JERRY *produces the mail from next door.*

JERRY. No idea. Look at these. Bills. Bills. Oh, by the way, letter for you.

  MARGO *hands him back the bills and opens the letter. Reads it.*

We could always go back upstairs? That's warmer. Or we can make it warmer.

MARGO. That's outrageous.

JERRY. Just a thought.

MARGO. Shut up, Jerry. This letter. This is disaster. This is a scandal. My worst fears have been realised.

JERRY. What are you talking about? Can we discuss this upstairs?

MARGO. They've announced the cast for the summer show. Listen. Maria – June Peebles!

JERRY. What, June from the office? With the...

MARGO (*clenched teeth*). Yes, Jerry. The same. And, oh, of course, Spotty Peggy Pilkington is still Liesl. And I'm... (*Reading down the list – incredulous.*) Sister Bertha!

JERRY. Well...

MARGO (*not to be mollified*). Oh, and look, Prudence has cast her own sister. Felicity Ferguson – Mother Abbess. This is not only wrong, it's *corrupt*. You have to stop this.

JERRY. How?

MARGO. All right, let's think. You're going to have to work on Sir. He'll have to work on Felicity, who'll have to work on Prudence.

JERRY. There's quite a few steps there.

MARGO. You can do it.

JERRY. And it's very delicate. Sir's been talking about restructuring at the firm and that could mean anything. Good for me, or bad for me, I don't know...

MARGO. Or, can June be transferred, somehow. Away, somewhere. Weren't you talking about JJM opening an Australian office?

JERRY (*ironically*). Or I suppose she could 'meet with an accident'?

MARGO (*seriously*). No, Jerry, that would be going too far. But, could you, do you think, do something… something to help. I'd be grateful.

MARGO *is suddenly uncharacteristically seductive.*

We've got nothing else to do this morning. They've got their hands full. The decorators have got their hands full. You could, you know, also…

JERRY. I've just got dressed. I've got a tie on.

MARGO. Well, that can be loosened.

JERRY. And there's a loom in there. It'll be… looming.

MARGO. Oh, just go to your shed then.

JERRY. What are you talking about? Come on, old girl, we've got to get warm, somehow.

MARGO. That's more like it. And you will think of something, won't you…?

They exit, to go upstairs…

TOM *suddenly bursts in, almost hysterical, followed by* BARBARA.

BARBARA. You heartless murdering bastard!

TOM. Sorry, Barbara, it's just the way things are.

BARBARA. Margo! Jerry! Where are you going? Stop him! He's a murderer.

MARGO. Barbara, what on earth is going on? Has he tried to attack you? I feared this might happen.

JERRY. Are you all right?

TOM. Of course she's all right, it's the pig.

BARBARA. Help me. Stop him. Where were you going?

MARGO *and* JERRY (*embarrassed*). We were, just, erm…

TOM. It's Pinky. She had seven.

MARGO. Seven?

BARBARA. Not seven, eight. But the last one is small and weak.

TOM. It's a runt, Barbara. (*To* JERRY.) It's called a runt.

JERRY. How very Anglo-Saxon.

BARBARA. Which you want to murder.

TOM. Come on. What do you expect me to do? Inflate it with a bicycle pump? I know it's rotten, but this sort of thing happens. It says so in the book – you sometimes get a runt in the litter. It's undersized, weak and excess to requirements, I'm afraid. Survival of the fittest.

JERRY. Can't Pinky help out?

TOM. Pinky's knackered. And she's not going to waste energy on something that's not going to make it anyway.

MARGO. So much for maternal instinct.

TOM. This is just that. This is Mother Nature, in action. This is Darwin. This trumps everything else.

BARBARA. So you're just going to let it die?

MARGO. You can't do that!

TOM. Now, Barbara, listen, listen, Margo, it's common sense. This is our livelihood, it's not a hobby. And it's not worth fighting a losing battle trying to keep it alive – it's just not efficient.

BARBARA. Damn your efficiency!

TOM. It's not my efficiency!

BARBARA. Yes it is your efficiency – it's becoming your god, and if you're going to turn into the kind of person that's going to let a little creature like that die just because it's efficient – then you can stuff it!

BARBARA *exits*.

MARGO. At last. The worm turns.

TOM. What do you mean?

MARGO. You've been bullying that poor girl for almost a year now. So you're overdue some home truths.

TOM. Bullying? She's been bullying me more like. I'm the one who's been wanting to backslide. And compromise. And she's been the one pushing me back up there. And anyway don't you talk to me about bullying. Jerry, help me out here.

JERRY. I'm not getting involved in... Ah!

MARGO. Ah. Aw...

BARBARA. Here we go.

These noises are being made because BARBARA has re-entered with the runt, wrapped in a tea towel. (We can only just see its head.) She places it with care on the breakfast table. It maybe emits a tiny squeal. The atmosphere changes to one of care and concentration.

Look at it.

JERRY. Poor little mite.

BARBARA. Sweet little thing. It's hardly breathing. (*Cradling it.*) There you go. Let's get some heat. And some food – or something. Tom? Tom?

TOM *looks at the runt. Then at* BARBARA, *then at* MARGO *and* JERRY*'s expectant faces.*

And makes a decision.

TOM. Right, we're going to need milk, brandy, something warm to wrap him in. Margo, get a towel from the bathroom. Jerry, bring the paraffin heater closer.

BARBARA (*lovingly*). Oh, Tom!

MARGO *exits.* JERRY *pulls the heater near.*

TOM. And something to help its breathing – what? Jerry?

JERRY. Oxygen?

TOM. Yes. Oxygen. Where do you get oxygen? The hospital? It's worth a go.

JERRY. What, Kingston General at the weekend? For a pig?

MARGO *returns with a fluffy towel.* BARBARA *carefully wraps the runt in it.*

MARGO. Couldn't we phone someone? A vet? The RSPCA?

TOM. No phone. Too expensive. And yours is still AWOL, right?

JERRY. I know someone who can help, with the oxygen. A few doors down. And I can phone from there if I can catch him.

JERRY *exits.*

TOM. Right, we're going to need milk, brandy. Margo, that's your job. Go next door and get some brandy.

MARGO. Of course, Tom.

MARGO *exits.*

MARGO *re-enters.*

MARGO. Courvoisier or Rémy Martin?

A look from TOM. *She re-exits.*

BARBARA. Is it too late to take it back, what I said? About you being heartless. And a bastard. And a murderer. I think you're a wonderful chap.

TOM. I'm sorry, it's the way I get. The dish runs away with the spoon sometimes. Now, even if Jerry finds some oxygen, how are we going to deliver it? We can't shove a tube down the poor thing's throat. We need to make something – a tent or something. (*Looks around.*)

BARBARA. How about using the germinating trays for the seeds?

TOM. Hang on, yes, that's brilliant!

They find a seed tray with a detachable Perspex lid and put it down on the table next to the runt.

He should fit in here nicely. There must be some way of sealing it up or making a hole or something. First we need to empty it out and clean it.

BARBARA. Okay. What about the cress?

TOM. Bugger the cress! This is an emergency.

BARBARA. I'll chuck it in the compost.

BARBARA scrapes the contents of the seed tray into the compost bin. TOM looks at the Perspex lid, holds it to the light to work out how it might be customised.

Re-enter JERRY with DR JOE, who also lives on the street. He is in full golf gear.

JERRY. Tom, Barbara, you know Dr Joe. I just caught him on the way to the golf.

DR JOE. The golf. But it's just started snowing. And I'm not a vet.

JERRY. He very kindly called a vet.

DR JOE. I'm not a vet.

JERRY. But there isn't a vet available. So we called his surgery.

DR JOE. I'm not there today because of –

BARBARA *and* TOM *and* JERRY. GOLF!

DR JOE (*points at his golf costume*). – but Mary, my receptionist, is.

TOM. Oxygen, what we need is oxygen.

DR JOE. That's what I'm trying to say, we have a spare cylinder at the surgery. Mary is driving it over.

BARBARA. But when? When?

DR JOE. She should be setting off now.

TOM. Could you have a look at the patient in the meanwhile?

DR JOE. I'm not a vet.

TOM. Yes, I think we've established that.

DR JOE gets out a stethoscope from his bag and listens to the runt's breathing. People stand back in a respectful semicircle.

MARGO rushes on with two bottles of brandy and a bottle of gold-top milk.

MARGO. I've got it!

Everybody shushes her as DR JOE *continues to examine the runt.*

Sorry.

Silence reigns.

And it's all looking nice next door.

ALL. Shush!

Silence.

MARGO. It's snowing out there.

ALL. Shush!

Silence.

DR JOE *finishes his examination and makes his diagnosis.*

DR JOE. Well, it's still breathing but only just. It's fighting for its life.

This has its effect on the assembled company. The couples draw closer to each other.

TOM. What's its chances?

DR JOE. Well, I'm not a vet.

TOM. I know you're not a fff–

JERRY (*intervening*). But in your professional opinion, Dr Joe.

DR JOE. Well, the oxygen is on its way. We have to find some way of distributing it.

TOM. Exactly.

DR JOE. But some sort of sustenance in the meanwhile...

MARGO. Look. I've got the brandy – (*Showing the bottles.*) I didn't know which so I brought both. And some milk. In the heat of the moment, I borrowed some from the milk float outside.

JERRY. You little tea-leaf.

BARBARA. You didn't have to, Margo, we've got milk here.

MARGO. No, Barbara, this is real milk. Unigate gold-top. We shouldn't be stinting on these things.

TOM. All right, Margo, heat it up. Where's that oxygen?

DR JOE (*looking at his watch*). It shouldn't be too long now. It's only a ten-minute drive. Even in snow.

BARBARA. Ten minutes!

TOM. Milk, Margo.

MARGO. I'm doing it.

> BARBARA *exits*. MARGO *pours the milk into a pan and puts it on the Aga*.
>
> *Enter a milkman in the unmistakable costume of peaked cap, white coat, etc. Except this is a lady milkman. Gruff and angry.*

MILKWOMAN. Where is she? Where is she?

TOM. Who are you?

MILKWOMAN. Who do you think I am? I'm Unigate. Some woman stole a pint from my float.

JERRY. Really?

MILKWOMAN. I was just delivering over the road there she was. Bold as brass. A drunk woman. Brandy bottles under her arm. And she ran in here. Have you seen her?

> JERRY *makes sure that the* MILKWOMAN *doesn't see* MARGO.

JERRY. We really don't know what you're talking about.

MILKWOMAN. We've been getting a lot of that lately. Alcoholics stealing milk after a big night out.

> MARGO *emerges from upstage*.

MARGO. How dare you!

MILKWOMAN. That's her! That's the alcoholic.

TOM. We can explain.

MILKWOMAN. You don't need to.

DR JOE. No, you don't understand. It's a medical emergency. We've got a patient here who needs urgent care.

MILKWOMAN (*still eyeing* MARGO *suspiciously*). Where?

TOM. Look.

Suddenly everyone is looking at the runt, who maybe gives a tiny squeal.

MILKWOMAN. It's a piglet.

BARBARA. And it's at death's door. Come on. We'll pay you back.

MILKWOMAN (*suddenly entranced*). Sweet little mite. (*To* JERRY.) Shall I help her warm it up? She may not be in a fit state.

JERRY. Who? What do you mean?

MILKWOMAN. The drunk woman.

JERRY. That's my wife.

MILKWOMAN (*compassionately*). That must be tough for you. For the whole family.

JERRY. How dare you!

TOM (*intervening*). Jerry, get some straw. From the thing.

JERRY. Straw? What thing?

TOM. From Geraldine's pen. Quickly.

JERRY *exits.*

BARBARA. How's the milk coming on?

MILKWOMAN. Shall I get some double cream?

DR JOE. That might be a bit rich.

MILKWOMAN. Of course, of course, you're the vet.

DR JOE. I'm not a vet.

TOM. Yes, good idea, get some cream. Single, though, not double.

MILKWOMAN. Righty-ho. (*To the pig.*) Hang on in there. (*Exits to get cream.*)

MARGO *has poured the warm milk into a bowl.*

MARGO. Is this too hot? Aren't you supposed to put your elbow in it?

TOM. Isn't that baby bathwater?

MARGO. I really have no idea, Tom. I need you to tell me what to do.

TOM. Try it with a teaspoon. If it's okay for you, it'll be okay for a pig. Hurry up, Margo!

MARGO *sips some milk from a teaspoon.*

MARGO. Delicious.

TOM. Yeah, that's fine, now pop some brandy in it.

MARGO. In what proportions?

TOM. It's not a cocktail party. Use your common sense!

MARGO *pours a tiny bit of each brandy into the milk and stirs it with a teaspoon. She approaches the runt with the teaspoon...*

BARBARA. She's breathing, but only just. Where's that oxygen.

DR JOE. Mary should be here by now. It's only round the...

MARY THE RECEPTIONIST *arrives, panting and out of breath (as she may well be after a quick quick-change) with a cylinder of oxygen on a trolley. Since it's pre-Christmas she has a Santa hat on. She is jolly but slightly eccentric.*

MARY. Doctor, doctor, I've got it.

DR JOE. Well done, Mary. You're an angel. Where is it?

MARY. It's in the car. It's a wee bit heavy.

TOM *takes charge.*

TOM. I'll go!

DR JOE. How did you get here so quickly?

MARY. You said it was an emergency, doctor. So I drove very fast.

DR JOE. Not dangerously, I hope.

MARY. I think it might have been a bit dangerous. There was a milk float – I might have just biffed it. Angry milkwoman gave me this – (*A carton of single cream.*)

MARGO. I'll take that. (*Examines the carton critically.*)

MARY. Anyway, I'm here now. Where's the patient?

DR JOE. Over here.

She is shown the runt and is instantly entranced.

MARY. Awh.

DR JOE. I know.

Enter JERRY *with a handful of straw. His clothes are muddied.*

JERRY. I've got the straw. Geraldine put up quite a fight.

MARGO (*who is adding cream to the milk*). We're throwing those slippers away.

JERRY. Who's this?

DR JOE. Mary, my receptionist.

BARBARA. She's brought the oxygen.

TOM. This oxygen!

DR JOE. Then my work here is done. I might just salvage a few holes. Last chance before Christmas. Let me know what happens. Bye, everyone.

ALL. Bye, doctor…

Exit DR JOE (*quick-change ahead!*).

TOM. Come on, Jerry, line the tray with straw. That's right. Now place the pig on the straw.

ALL *help taking the runt from the towel and placing it very gently on the straw in the seed tray.*

TOM *holds the lid of the seed tray.*

Now all we need to do is to seal it up somehow.

JERRY. We need to block up those little holes.

MARY. Sellotape, have you got any Sellotape?

BARBARA. Somewhere. (*Opens drawers randomly.*)

TOM. And make a big hole for the tubing. The tubing. The tubing. (*To* MARY.) Did you bring any tubing?

MARY. The doctor didn't tell me to. Oh no… have I done something wrong?

JERRY. Not at all. You've been a godsend.

TOM. Margo, don't just stand there gawping – get that stuff down that pig.

MARGO. Very well. Stand back everybody. (*Has a teaspoon and proceeds to try and feed the runt.*)

ALL *hold their breath as the milk and brandy mixture is fed to the runt. A collective sigh as it seems to be responding.*

There you go.

BARBARA. That's it.

MARY. Awh.

TOM. Don't faff about, Margo, get on with it.

MARGO. Sorry, Tom, I'll do this my way. (*Feeds the pig.*) A tip for the future, Barbara, always feed a piglet from the corner of his mouth.

BARBARA. Thanks, Margo, I'll remember that.

JERRY. Well whatever happens the bacon will certainly taste nice.

MARGO. Jerry, don't be an ass.

JERRY. Just thinking ahead.

A POLICEMAN *enters with an intercom on his lapel. His has an open notebook.*

TOM. Hello, can I help you?

POLICEMAN. Is that your car that's parked outside? And when I say parked, I mean left halfway up the kerb with its doors open.

MARY. No, constable, I'm afraid that's mine.

POLICEMAN. Quite a journey we've had, miss. I could hardly keep up. (*Opens notebook.*) Sixty miles an hour in a residential area, in fresh snow – two red lights, and one milk-float that will never be quite the same.

TOM. No, you don't understand, constable.

POLICEMAN. Sorry, sir, what is it that I don't understand?

MARY. It was a matter of life and death.

POLICEMAN. It certainly was the way you were driving.

MARY. Oh dear.

BARBARA. Listen, please. I know this sounds unlikely, but our pig's just had a litter – and there's this little tiny runt and if we hadn't got any oxygen for him he would have died. And he still may. Look.

POLICEMAN. Well I'm not sure that's any excuse for... (*Sees the pig and is immediately entranced.*) Aw. Poor little thing. Why didn't you tell me this straight away? Right, what's the plan? How can I help?

BARBARA. We have the oxygen...

TOM. And all we need to do is to put this on here...

BARBARA. Seal it up, make a hole...

TOM. And pipe the oxygen in somehow.

POLICEMAN. Yes but how? Right.

MARGO. How refreshing to see you don't devote all your energies to shepherding people on when they park outside Surbiton public library for a couple of minutes.

JERRY. Give it a rest, Margo.

POLICEMAN (*ignoring this*). Tubing, we need some tubing.

MARY. He didn't tell me to bring any.

POLICEMAN. I'll radio back to the station. The boys will
know.

The POLICEMAN *goes to one side and radios in.*

We may overhear the odd word. MARY *is looking at the
runt, but casting the odd glance at the* POLICEMAN.

TOM. Thinking caps, everyone. Tubing.

MARY. I know. Maybe there are some milk-straws on the float.
Maybe I could catch it up. It won't be going fast... (*This is
plainly a terrible idea.*) No. Terrible idea. Sorry.

POLICEMAN (*on radio, to one side*). Yes, sarge. A pig. Not
breathing. We've got ox... yes, we've got oxygen, but we
don't know how to connect it up... Yes. Yes.

BARBARA. I've got it. We've got the rubber tubes we use to
siphon up the wine.

JERRY. That bacon sounds better and better.

TOM. Wrong gauge.

MARGO. Jerry.

POLICEMAN (*to the radio*). Thanks, sarge. I will. (*To* JERRY.)
Have you got a car, sir?

JERRY. Yes, of course, the Volvo 265.

POLICEMAN. The one outside?

JERRY. Yes, she's a beauty, isn't she?

POLICEMAN. Perfect. We'll rip the tubing out of your front end.

JERRY. Like hell you will.

POLICEMAN. Yep. The overflow pipe from the radiator.
Come on.

JERRY. Over my dead body.

MARGO. Jerry, don't be an ass, do what you're told.

POLICEMAN. Come on, quick, I'll give you a hand.

JERRY (*heroically*.) I can do this on my own.

BARBARA. Bravo, Jerry.

TOM. Thanks, Jerry.

MARGO. Well done, Jerry.

   JERRY *harrumphs and exits*.

MARY. I've got the Sellotape.

TOM. Good. Seal up the little holes.

   MARY *tears off Sellotape strips*.

BARBARA. Scissors.

POLICEMAN. Scissors.

MARY. Scissors. Thank you.

TOM. Now seal up the air holes. Leave one open for the air flow. That's right.

   MARY *does so*.

POLICEMAN. Nice work.

MARY. I am St John's Ambulance.

POLICEMAN. Really? Well it's paying off...

BARBARA. That's quite enough flirting from you two. Even if we get tubing we'll still need to deliver the oxygen somehow.

POLICEMAN. Tools. You need tools to make a hole. Like a bradawl or a gimlet.

BARBARA. Next door, Margo. Get something from next door.

MARGO. I'm not stopping them working.

POLICEMAN. I'll go.

   Exit POLICEMAN.

MARY. I'll go too.

TOM. No, Mary, we need you here to administer the oxygen. You've done that before? St John's Ambulance.

MARY. Yes, of course. Not with pigs, obviously, but yes.

TOM. Good. Come on...

BARBARA. What's keeping Jerry?

TOM. Come on...

Enter JERRY *with a tangle of tubes, plainly ripped out of his car.*

JERRY. Here we go.

MARGO. It's like *The Sound of Music*!

JERRY. Margo, get a grip. I've buggered up the Volvo for you.

MARGO. Not for me, Jerry for... (*Indicates the runt.*) Do you give them names?

Enter POLICEMAN, *carrying various tools.*

POLICEMAN. Okay, I've got screwdrivers. Lots of them.

MARGO. They weren't using them, were they?

BARBARA. Can you smash a hole through?

TOM. No, it's got to be tight for the tubing. Jerry, get that tubing straightened out.

JERRY. On it.

POLICEMAN. I know – we'll melt it through. Can you heat this up?

BARBARA. We've got an Aga.

POLICEMAN. No, a flame, a naked flame. You've got any candles?

BARBARA looks for candles.

BARBARA. Yes. Candles, candles...

MARY. I've got a cigarette lighter.

POLICEMAN. Oh, you smoke, do you?

MARY. Just after work sometimes – in the evenings.

POLICEMAN. Oh, me too, sometimes. Shouldn't really.

BARBARA *has a pair of home-made candles.*

BARBARA. Here you go.

POLICEMAN. What are they?

BARBARA. Candles. We make our own. They do work. (*To*
MARY.) Go on, light them.

MARY *does so with her lighter.*

POLICEMAN. Nicely done. Now I just need to heat this thing up.

TOM. How's the tubing coming on?

JERRY. Done. My poor Volvo.

BARBARA. Thank you, Jerry.

TOM. Come on. We have the oxygen, we have the incubator.
We have the tubing. Just to get it in...

MARGO. Tom...

The POLICEMAN *is heating the screwdriver in the candle
flames.*

POLICEMAN. Just be patient.

MARY (*staring, transfixed at the capable* POLICEMAN).
Getting there. Getting hotter. Good work, erm...

POLICEMAN. Frank.

MARY. Mary.

MARGO. Jerry. (*Looking at the pig.*) Hurry up, hurry. It's not
moving.

POLICEMAN. Can't rush this.

MARY. Frank's right.

MARGO. Barbara.

POLICEMAN. Okay. That should be hot enough. Stand back.

POLICEMAN *pushes the hot screwdriver into the Perspex, making a hole, which he matches to the bore of the tubing from the car.*

That should do it.

TOM. Let me just attach this.

MARY. I'll do the other end.

MARGO. It's not moving.

POLICEMAN. Go on, Mary.

MARY. Okay, Frank.

BARBARA. She's not moving.

TOM. Right. Well. Come on. There we go.

BARBARA. There we go, darling.

MARGO. Careful.

MARY. Gently does it.

She attaches the free end of the tubing to the oxygen cylinder.

Ready.

TOM. Okay. Now be careful. A low setting at first.

MARY. Okay. And go...

She turns a wheel. Checking dials, etc., carefully.

Silence.

Then... we hear a slight hiss as the makeshift respirator starts to work.

JERRY. Here we go.

All eyes on the runt in its straw. Lights change. Almost as if a light is coming from the manger. An almost religious silence. BARBARA *hands the extra candle to* TOM, *next to her.*

MARGO. It's still not moving.

TOM. Wait.

POLICEMAN. Little bit stronger. Just a tidge.

MARY. All right.

POLICEMAN. Take your time.

MARY. Here we go.

JERRY. Come on.

BARBARA. Not too much. It's only tiny.

POLICEMAN. It'll be fine.

MARY. A tidge more? Here we go.

Suddenly.

TOM. Look. Look.

JERRY. Look. It's stirring.

MARGO. Jerry! It's fighting. Fighting for its life.

BARBARA. Come on, darling. You can do it. You can do it.

POLICEMAN. That's a brave little pig.

MARY. Come on, sweetheart.

TOM. It's breathing. Everyone, it's breathing. I think it's going to pull through.

BARBARA. It's going to live. Oh, Tom.

MARGO. Jerry. Look.

JERRY. I know.

ALL *are delighted.* POLICEMAN*'s radio crackles.*

POLICEMAN. Hello, sarge? Yes. It's teas all round in the canteen.

We might hear distant cheers from the radio.

Over. Yes, I will. Over and out. (*To the company.*) My sarge and the boys at the station say all the best.

Again silence as they observe the miracle.

TOM and BARBARA *holding candles.* JERRY *with his arm around* MARGO. *The* POLICEMAN, *we notice, is standing close to* MARY.

It's basically a nativity tableau.

In the distance we hear carol singers. 'O Little Town of Bethlehem'. It starts snowing.

Suddenly TOM *speaks.*

TOM. Margo.

MARGO. Yes?

TOM. No. (*Indicating the runt.*) Margo…

A slow smile from MARGO.

Lights fade.

As the set revolves, we hear a full-blown orchestral version of 'The Sound of Music'.

ACT FOUR

'After-party'

Summer

*We arrive at the Leadbetters'. The house is fully redecorated.
New wallpaper. The furniture rearranged. (No Hammond Organ.)*

*The house is set up for a large gathering. Many bottles of
Champagne – with glasses at the ready. A sideboard groaning
with buffet food. Since it is set up for the first-night party of* The
Sound of Music, *maybe suitable decorations. 'SOUND OF
MUSIC, JUNE 1977' on a banner. The music we hear is, in fact,
coming from a radiogram.*

TOM *and* BARBARA *are sitting waiting. (If there is time for
the quickest of changes they maybe in posher clothes.)*

TOM. They'll all be here any minute.

BARBARA. Yes. They will. Wow. What are we going to say?

TOM. I mean… (*Pause.*) That was *The Sound of Music*, wasn't it?

BARBARA. Possibly.

TOM. Just checking. Some of it seemed familiar certainly.

BARBARA. Didn't get off to a great start, did it?

TOM. You mean the mountain falling over? Not really.

BARBARA. And Margo did seem to be in a different key to the
band.

TOM. It's a hard song to sing, though. When you're holding a
mountain up.

BARBARA. Mind you the band were in quite a few different
keys themselves.

A pause. Then they giggle.

We have to be supportive.

TOM. Of course. Of course.

Pause.

BARBARA. What about her making up the words in 'Favourite Things'.

TOM. Stop it.

BARBARA. And that child.

TOM. Which one?

BARBARA. I think this evening we'll just concentrate on Margo and Jerry, shall we? And not say anything about us. Not tonight.

TOM. Good plan. Are we allowed to open the Champagne yet?

BARBARA. Not yet, maybe. Not till Jerry's here.

TOM. I didn't think Margo was going to be Maria, originally, was she? Wasn't someone else cast?

BARBARA. Yes. June. From JJM.

TOM. What happened.

BARBARA. She ran away to Spain. With the pro from the tennis club.

TOM. Ah. Shame.

BARBARA. Pablo.

TOM. Ah.

JERRY *enters. Dinner jacket, ruched shirt-front.*

TOM *and* BARBARA (*overly jolly*). Jerry!

JERRY (*determinedly jolly*). I know, I know. We've just got to get through this. The mood in the hall was pretty tricky so I've come on ahead. Margo's got her party frock in her dressing room, so she'll be... And look we've got Champagne. Lots of Champagne. Tom? I'm going to.

TOM. Well, if you are.

JERRY. We definitely need it. Barbara?

BARBARA. Just juice for me, thanks, Jerry.

Pause for drinks – served and sipped. JERRY *drinks his at a gulp and refills automatically.*

JERRY. Well, let's say there were a few gremlins this evening. Let's say that.

TOM. Maybe they'll be ironed out. There's another performance tomorrow.

JERRY. Jesus.

BARBARA. Still, one can't expect an amateur production to be perfect, can one?

JERRY. Not after tonight.

BARBARA. And I'm sure they can fix the mountain. And repair the footlights. And find a couple more children.

JERRY. The audience were pretty restless, has to be said. I thought Prudence was going to explode.

BARBARA. Did you notice Mary and her policeman boyfriend there?

TOM. Not after the interval, they weren't. And was that the Lord Mayor, with the chains on? He kept on rattling in and out. Is he incontinent?

JERRY. Could be. I think maybe Gretl was – at least onstage. I think that's what blew up the footlights.

BARBARA. Oh dear. Poor mite.

TOM. I presume that was her mother who ran on...

They laugh, in spite of themselves.

BARBARA. And Felicity didn't, let's be honest, when we got there, quite have the high notes for 'Climb Ev'ry Mountain'. Or indeed the low notes.

TOM. Or any in between. The interval was very welcome for quite a few of us.

JERRY. Yes. Tricky. My boss's wife. Not to mention my own wife. Tonight will be an interesting work-life challenge. And

Andrew. All his talk of the firm being 'restructured' – and 'imminent announcements'. I've no idea what that means – certainly for me. Let's face it, I could be out on my ear.

TOM. Well, you and Margo could always go self-sufficient. Sorry, bad joke, bad timing, sorry.

JERRY. It may even come to that. Could do worse.

TOM. You could always share our goat.

We hear a noise off.

JERRY. Shush, shush. Here they come, here they come.

JERRY, TOM *and* BARBARA *stand in line and applaud* MARGO *as she enters, looking ravishing.*

JERRY, TOM *and* BARBARA. Brava! Brava! (*Etc.*)

MARGO (*giving nothing away*). Good evening.

BARBARA. Where's the rest of the company?

MARGO. Nobody's coming.

JERRY. What?

TOM. Really?

MARGO. Nobody.

BARBARA. Oh no, no. Margo.

TOM (*doing his best*). Well… Fine. Let them do what they like. The show had a few… issues… maybe. But you, Margo, you were… you were… didn't I say, Barbara.

BARBARA. Yes, you did… you did… and I agreed.

TOM. And I'll say it again. A few mistakes indeed but you were really… really… you were really…

MARGO (*factual*). Bloody awful.

BARBARA. Oh come on!

MARGO. Well I was.

BARBARA. Come on, you can't take *all* the blame – the rest of the cast were pretty awful… I mean…

MARGO. As well. You were going to say as well. And you're right. But I was the leading lady. I could have saved that show.

TOM. No human being could have.

MARGO. But I gave a performance that plumbed the depths of ineptitude.

It's truth time.

TOM (*deep breath*). Yes, Margo, yes. You were terrible.

MARGO. Thank you, Tom. I appreciate your honesty.

JERRY. But there's always tomorrow night.

MARGO. There isn't.

BARBARA. What?

MARGO. We've been taken off. The Mayor says the show would give the borough a bad name.

TOM. I noticed he was unhappy.

MARGO. And they wouldn't have been able to repair the set anyway. And Sister Sophia injured herself falling into the pit.

JERRY. Will she be all right?

MARGO. Yes. I'm not sure the timpani will though.

BARBARA. What about the people who have bought tickets?

MARGO. They've told everyone that the chandelier is unsafe. They've gone dark. Prudence is still there, consoling parents, administering first aid. No one's exactly in a party mood.

JERRY. Just us then. Champagne, darling?

MARGO. Yes please. I need it.

JERRY. Tom? Barbara?

TOM. I'm fine.

BARBARA. I'm on the juice, thanks.

Silence. All eyes turn to the food.

JERRY. There's lots of food. (*Pause.*) Thanks, Tom, Barbara, for that.

Another silence.

MARGO (*referring to 'The Sound of Music', which is still playing on the radiogram*). Can we turn that off now, please?

JERRY. Of course.

He does so.

MARGO (*referring to the banner*). And maybe take that down...

TOM. I'm on it.

Suddenly – a distant 'ding-dong'.

JERRY (*exiting*). Who's that?

MARGO. I hope it's not the photographer from the *Surbiton Sentinel*. I tried to get him cancelled.

JERRY (*re-entering*). Look, it's Andrew and Felicity.

And so it is. Both dressed up to the nines. Surprisingly good-humoured.

MARGO. How sweet of you to come.

SIR. I know it's been quite a night, but we didn't want to desert our friends. Margo, Jerry, Barbara, and... er...

TOM. Tom.

SIR. Quite so.

JERRY. We have Champagne. And lots of yummy food.

FELICITY *and* SIR. Ooh, don't mind if we do. Just a snifter... (*Etc.*)

JERRY serves and tops up drinks during the following. MARGO accepts absent-mindedly. Still a 'no' from BARBARA.

MARGO. So how is everyone?

FELICITY. Mostly gone home. Prudence is inconsolable. Says it's partly her fault.

MARGO. Only partly?

FELICITY. Well she seems to have had enough of the Players. Says she was never valued or appreciated.

MARGO. Well she may have a point there.

FELICITY. I should never have agreed to be cast.

BARBARA. You did very well. On your duet, anyway 'Favourite Things'.

MARGO. I panicked, sorry. I was just making up words.

TOM. Yes, it's a bad song to forget the words in!

FELICITY (*good-humouredly*). Yes. 'Kippers for breakfast and weekends in Paris' did rather throw me.

They all laugh.

MARGO. Well they *are* my favourite things. I was trying to be in the moment!

SIR. Well I for one – and I hope I'm not speaking out of turn – am glad it's all over. Home has been hell.

JERRY. Hear hear.

MARGO. Jerry!

JERRY. Well, it's been tough, let's agree. But it's all over now.

SIR. That and my health, and many other factors have made me think deeply about life and work – and the future of JJM.

JERRY. Ah.

SIR. So, one of the reasons I wanted to be here was to make an announcement. I didn't want you to hear about it in the workplace, Jerry.

JERRY. Right... appreciated. So...

SIR. So, the big bosses in Amsterdam have decided to expand JJM. And to that end, and partially as a result of the success of the marsupial range, they are opening an Australian office. In Sydney.

JERRY. Ah...

SIR. Which, I have decided, after long consideration, that I will open and run. Felicity and I are flying to our new home in the autumn.

ALL. Wonderful. Bravo. How exciting. (*Etc.*)

SIR. It's a great new adventure for JJM and for us both.

FELICITY. And he needs to slow down a bit. His heart.

SIR. My heart is fine.

FELICITY. Of course.

SIR. Nothing wrong with me.

JERRY. But that's wonderful, Sir.

TOM. Yes. Well done, Sir.

SIR. Thanks, Jerry, thanks, erm… Tom.

TOM. Quite so.

SIR. What?

JERRY. But, Sir, Sir, I have to ask… what about here? JJM Sydney, fine dandy and dinkum, but what about JJM Purley? How can it be run without you?

SIR. Well I'll tell you how. By *you*, Jerry, that's how. By you. I've cleared it with the Dutch, and my job is your job, if you want it.

JERRY. If I want it? If I want it? Of course I do, Sir, thanks so much. I won't let you down.

SIR. I know.

MARGO. Jerry. Wonderful.

Handshakes all round.

BARBARA. And quite right too.

TOM. Well done, old chap. Bravo!

JERRY. Let's all drink to that.

More drinks.

MARGO. Excuse me. I also have an announcement to make. After this evening, I have decided to retire from show business.

ALL. Oh no…

MARGO. I've been thinking for a while now that so many women haven't a clue what to wear – no offence, Barbara, no offence, Felicity – so I intend, with Jerry's help (thank you, Jerry) to start a fashion consultancy for the suburban woman. I'm thinking, 'Mystique – by Margo'.

JERRY. Good heavens. I…

MARGO. And never again let it be said that I contribute nothing to this household…

JERRY. Erm, I don't think anyone actually ever said that.

TOM (*saving the day*). Well I think it's marvellous.

BARBARA. So do I.

TOM. And I suggest a toast. A toast. Here's to new beginnings.

JERRY. New beginnings! (*To* SIR.) You're going to start a new firm.

FELICITY. And we're going to start a new life.

MARGO. And I'm going to start a new business.

JERRY. And I'm going to be a managing director.

BARBARA. And I'm going to have a baby.

JERRY. And Tom can come back and work for JJM, just part time, of course, but the firm can't really thrive without… Sorry, what did you say.

TOM. We're going to have a baby.

MARGO. What?… When? And *how*?

TOM. Trust me, it was the work of a moment.

JERRY. Barbara, Tom, this is…

MARGO *and* JERRY (*together*). Wonderful.

BARBARA. I know. It is. Quite wonderful. (*Looks around at her friends*.) And you know what? Life is good.

There is a pause as the two couples stare at each other. Then they pile in for a group hug and celebration – handshakes and hugs from FELICITY *and* SIR.

The unmistakable theme music from The Good Life *is heard and covers their general jubilation as the curtain falls.*

The End.

www.nickhernbooks.co.uk

facebook.com/nickhernbooks

twitter.com/nickhernbooks